THE COMPLETE BOOK *of*
HOME
ORGANIZATION

THE COMPLETE BOOK of
HOME
ORGANIZATION

by Toni Hammersley

weldon**owen**

PART ONE
Kitchen + Dining

PART TWO
Living + Storage

PART THREE
Working + Outdoor

Within the walls of our home, we try to live a balanced life. Most days, the dog is chasing the cat and dinner is bubbling over on the stovetop. Piles of dirty laundry, a sink full of dishes, and unmade beds are screaming for attention. And in between the chaotic days, when life slows down a bit, you may see carpet lines, a polished refrigerator door with no signs of fingerprints, and a glimpse of order peeking out from the pantry. Balance, not perfection, is the key to a happy home. In this book, I am going to teach you how to maintain balance in your home and regain the love you felt when you first claimed it as your own.

We will go through each space, combing through the unknown, purging, donating, and categorizing. I will offer weekly challenges, including checklists, to make the tasks more enjoyable and easier to tackle. Each challenge gives much-needed attention to an area of the home, beginning with the kitchen. I'll offer solutions to common organizing problems and share pictures that will inspire you to stay focused. By the end of the book, the clutter will be gone, and order will have finally found your home once again.

It's time to tackle the messes and take back your space. Take as long as you need to complete each challenge, and refer back to this book when you need inspiration. And remember, the journey is the destination.

Hugs,
Toni

Kitchen+Dining

My favorite room in our house is the kitchen. This space allows me to express my creativity through decorating, organizing, cooking, and baking. Over the years, it has evolved from complete chaos to a fine-tuned and systematically organized space. Through trial and error, I've been able to implement new systems to make it work for my family—and throughout this chapter I'll be sharing ways that your kitchen can work for you. However small or abundant your space may be, there's no doubt you can make the most of it. Next, we'll hit the dining room—a space not to be forgotten. By weaving these two spaces together and incorporating as many organizing solutions as you can, you'll be able to simplify the clutter and perfect your storage so that you can enjoy these rooms to the fullest.

001 REINVENT YOUR KITCHEN

The kitchen is the heart of the home, and a well-planned space will streamline food prep, cooking, baking, and cleaning—all while maximizing time and efficiency. Before you start pulling everything out of the cabinets and drawers, begin by writing out a plan. Consider how many cabinets and drawers you have. What needs organizing? Which areas are used for which tasks? How many gadgets, small appliances, and dishes can you purge, and how much space will result? Write out your ideas and get a detailed plan on paper. Once you've got your guideline, it's time to get started.

002 DIVIDE INTO ZONES

The kitchen functions at its best when it's set up in zones. There are five main zones: cooking, preparation, cleaning, storage, and food. Everything in your kitchen should fit into one of these five categories. If you have an item that doesn't fit, it may not belong in the kitchen.

A. COOKING Your cooking space should include spices, oils and vinegars, cooking utensils, pots and pans, pot holders, trivets, and other tools.

B. CLEANING All things related to cleaning your kitchen should be in this zone, which is typically centered around the dishwasher and kitchen sink. Categories include kitchen cleaners, under the sink items (sponges, paper towels, microfiber cloths, trash bags, dishwasher detergent), recycling bins, and trash cans.

C. PREPARATION Everything needed to prep meals goes in the preparation zone. Items might include mixing bowls, knives, cutting boards, kitchen gadgets, blender, and other appliances. Specific areas will form within this zone, like the baking and school lunch stations (see items 015, 047).

D. STORAGE Items in the storage zone include food containers, silverware, dishes, glasses, and small appliances.

E. FOOD The pantry is considered the food zone. If you don't have a pantry, designate a few cupboards or a standing cabinet in which to store food items.

Kitchen islands are excellent multipurpose areas that might serve as storage, preparation, or cooking spaces.

004

MAKE A DIY SINK CLEANER

Some studies state a higher concentration of bacteria can be found in the kitchen sink than in the toilet bowl. Here's my recipe for an easy kitchen sink cleanser that you can DIY at home and use on a daily basis to keep the germs away.

YOU'LL NEED

1 clean spray bottle
1 part white vinegar
1 part water

DIRECTIONS

Mix the vinegar and water, cap your bottle, and shake vigorously. Use a permanent marker to label it "Daily Sink Cleaner"—this will prevent confusion with other sprays and remind you of its usefulness! Simply spray your sink and faucet, let sit for a few minutes, then wipe down. You'll have a fresher sink in no time.

003

END YOUR DAY WITH A CLEAN KITCHEN

Few things feel better than waking up to a clean space. At the end of each day, when dinner is done and the kids are in bed, take 15 minutes to give everything a quick cleanup and wipe-down. You'll notice that this easy task will really affect your mood for the rest of the evening—and make heading into the next day's meal preparations a breeze.

LOAD Load the dishwasher (and empty it the next morning—now you'll always know whether it's clean or dirty).

CLEAN Clean the sink: Rinse out any remaining food, scrub with baking soda, and use a daily cleaning solution (see item 004). You should do a separate deep clean on the sink once per week.

SPRAY Spray and wipe down the countertops, stovetop, table, and any other surfaces.

REPLACE Put a clean washcloth and dish towel out and toss the dirty ones in the laundry.

EMPTY Take the garbage out to avoid old food smells and leaks, and put a new liner in the can.

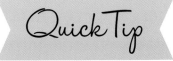

Quick Tip

USE BAKING SODA AND LEMON

Baking soda may be the unsung hero of keeping your home fresh and clean. To make an easy pantry-sourced compound, use half of a lemon with some baking soda to create an abrasive scrubber.

This combo also works on rust stains on porcelain tubs—and many other seemingly tough cleaning jobs. The lemon also helps whiten or "bleach" areas that are yellowed.

You'll be surprised how easily—and naturally—the markings will lift off.

005

CLEAN OUT YOUR SPICES

Spices are the soul of any home-cooked meal, and having them easily accessible makes cooking that much more fun. Create an organized spice station near your cooking area to store your spices, oils, and mixes. Remember that the key is functional organizing, so you will want this space to be near your oven. It's time to toss out those ten-year-old spices and replenish them with fresh, new jars.

REMOVE Pull out all the spices and condiments from your cabinets, pantry, and drawers so you can take inventory of what you have. Throw out all expired items—the flavor won't last.

CATEGORIZE Sort by size and type of item (cooking oils, cooking spices, baking spices, mixes, etc.)

ORGANIZE Stack your remaining jars on spice shelves, in drawers, or on lazy susans, or section them into baskets as best suits your needs. Alphabetize if it helps you find spices more easily.

DESIGNATE Choose a space near your oven where you can keep oils, vinegars, and other commonly used items (see item 006, at right).

006

CREATE A "BEST OF" STATION

It's great to have a station on your counter where you keep your favorite cooking essentials. Olive oil, vinegar, salt, pepper, and garlic are the most commonly used cooking ingredients.

Keeping them within arm's reach of your cooking space will make using them easier and more cook-friendly. You can repurpose an old cutting board or cheese tray to designate this space.

007

THINK OUTSIDE THE SHELF

My top two favorite spice organizers are lazy susans and drawers. No cabinet space needed!

Use multiple lazy susans to organize spices by category, such as baking spices, cooking spices, spice mixes, and seasonings. You'll find them faster when you know which type you're looking for.

If you're lacking cabinet space, store spices in a kitchen drawer. This method will require you to purchase spice

jars, but it's an effective organizational method and should appeal to those who like uniformity. Make sure you measure the height of the jars and drawers before purchasing. You can even go one step further and organize your spice drawer alphabetically. It sounds crazy, but it will make your life easier.

If you are switching your spices into new containers, don't forget to label the bottom of the jars with the expiration date.

008
GROUP YOUR UTENSILS

Create a functional, organized kitchen space by grouping utensils together and categorizing them by their various uses.

CLEAN Clear out all of your utensil drawers and wipe them down.

PURGE Donate or get rid of utensils that you haven't used in the last 12 months.

GATHER Group containers and other items into categories.

CREATE Use jars, baskets, or bins on your counter—or style out an existing drawer. Crock pots are great for storing your most commonly used utensils—they hold a lot and they're easy to grab. Keep various crocks within easy reach on your counter.

MEASURING TOOLS If you keep them all together, there's no digging around when you want to use one. If you're short on space, you can hang these on a cabinet door (adhesive hooks are great for this).

CUTTING TOOLS Knives, mezzaluna, cheese cutter, apple slicer, sandwich cutter, scissors—it's nice to have all of the sharps in one careful drawer.

009
UTILIZE YOUR DRAWERS

As you clean and categorize, remember to purge what you don't need—be ruthless! It will give you the extra space for the things you do need. Use your kitchen drawers to group together the items you will be using, as follows.

COMMON ITEMS Keep certain heavy-use items handy like can openers and rubber scrapers, and include others depending on your cooking habits—maybe the guacamole tools, peelers and slicers, or tea items.

LESS COMMON ITEMS Special-occasion or recipe items like pastry tools, graters, and temperature gadgets aren't going to come out every day, but you'll know where they are when you do need one.

012 KEEP DISHES NEAR THE SINK

Storing dishes in cabinets near the dishwasher makes for easy loading and unloading. Use wire racks to create multilevel, makeshift shelving for more storage. It may actually free up your cabinet space, too! Purge dishes that are chipped and any you no longer use. Most kitchen space issues come from storing dishes and items that are no longer in use.

010 SEPARATE LIDS FROM BASES

Whether you prefer plastic or glass, most food storage containers consist of two pieces: the base and the lid. Gain control of this area by storing lids separately, in a designated basket or tucked inside a hanging door organizer. Maximize the remaining space by sorting and stacking reusable containers by size.

011 STORE POTS AND PANS CREATIVELY

Pots and pans can become the bane of your existence thanks to how difficult they are to keep organized. There are a few methods for storing them: hang them on a rail, slide them into multilevel wire racks, store them on an open shelf, or stack them in a cabinet. Depending on how much money you want to spend, you can even find some fancy systems at home improvement stores. For an inexpensive option, use vertical slotted file organizers (designed for office use) to store baking sheets, racks, and muffin pans.

Quick Tip

TOTE IT!

If you're short on space, organize paper goods and utensils in a cute metal caddy. For a cookout, just grab the caddy and head outside.

013
DECLUTTER COUNTERS

Is anything better than walking into your kitchen and seeing a nice, clean space for cooking? Maybe a few things, but there's nothing worse than the reverse—heading into the kitchen to start dinner, tired after a long day, and you can't even get meal prep started until you tidy up your countertops.

As we all know, clutter begets clutter. It's a self-fulfilling prophecy. But if you take a good hard look at what is currently taking up real estate on your counters, you'll be able to find creative relocation solutions. And a clutter-free, cook-ready kitchen can once again be yours for the taking.

KNIVES Toss the bulky wooden knife organizer. Hang knives on a magnetic strip.

POTS AND PANS Hang pots and pans on the wall or store them on an open shelf.

BASKETS Stash those pesky vitamins and medicine bottles away in a cute wicker basket.

BREAD BOX Store loaves of bread in a cute enamelware bread box.

014
MAINTAIN ORDER

Maintaining a routine and cleaning the kitchen as you go is one of the hardest habits to get into—but once you've got the hang of it, you'll wonder why you weren't doing it this way the whole time. It may be hard to get started, but in the long run, it saves you work.

Make it a point to wash your dishes right after you use them. Either put them in the dishwasher and run it each evening when full, or take a couple of minutes to wash them by hand.

If you don't already, wash your kitchen floor once a week. It doesn't have to be a deep cleaning—just sweep up the big crumbs with a broom and give it a light mopping.

Finally, designate five minutes a day to put things away. Remove anything that doesn't belong in the kitchen, on the counters or out in the open. Pack lunches, defrost meat for tomorrow's dinner, and prep breakfast for the morning. It will feel good—I promise.

015
DESIGN A BAKING STATION

Do you have a certain area in your kitchen where you whip together delicious cookies or homemade bread? Keeping all of your ingredients within arm's reach of your preparation area will make you feel like a gourmet pastry chef.

You don't need a pull-out drawer to create this space. Any cabinet will do, as long as your ingredients are corralled together and located close to where you prepare your recipes.

In order to use every bit of space you've got, hang your pot holders on a Command hook mounted inside the cabinet door.

STEP ONE Pull out all of your baking ingredients (see item 016) and check the expiration dates.

STEP TWO Make a list of missing ingredients and go shopping for needed items.

STEP THREE Clear out a kitchen cabinet, shelf, or drawer that will be used as your baking station.

STEP FOUR Label your containers and stock your new space. You can use any type of container to create an organized baking space. I chose OXO containers—they're easy to open when your hands are messy and they fit well together. Another idea would be mason jars. Your favorite mixing bowls should also find their way to your new station.

016
STOCK YOUR BAKING CABINET WITH THE BASICS

If you're a baker—whether aspiring or accomplished—you likely have a lot of ingredients on hand. Use this checklist to fill your containers.

LARGE CONTAINERS
☐ All-purpose flour
☐ Self-rising flour
☐ Bread flour
☐ Powdered sugar
☐ Old-fashioned oats
☐ Quick-cooking oats
☐ Granulated sugar

MEDIUM CONTAINERS
☐ Light brown sugar
☐ Dark brown sugar
☐ Chocolate chips
☐ Bisquick mix

SMALL CONTAINERS
☐ Cocoa powder
☐ Raisins
☐ Baking chocolate bars
☐ Baking powder
☐ Baking soda
☐ Yeast (individually packaged)
☐ Cornstarch

017 DESIGNATE A DRINK STATION

If you're a coffee lover, it's quite easy to save yourself both time and money by creating a mini coffee shop right in your very own kitchen! Find a spot, either on your countertop or on a stand or hutch, that you can use as a station, and start gathering your favorite drinks and supplies. It's easy and the rewards are fabulous.

A. TEA OR COFFEE POT You don't need an expensive coffee machine to make this space special. Whether you prefer a coffee urn, teapot, individual brewer, traditional coffee maker, or a grand espresso machine with all the bells and whistles, it will work just fine as a focal point for this project.

B. MUGS AND CUPS Keep your most-used mugs handy. Put them on a pretty tray to add some flair.

C. COFFEE AND TEA If your machine doesn't store coffee beans, keep your grounds, beans, or K-cups in a large (sealable) jar at your coffee station. Tea often comes in pretty packages that look great when displayed, so don't worry about having to hide anything.

D. CONDIMENTS Finding unique vessels to keep your sugar, cream, and honey in will make every day feel special. Look for matching condiment sets online.

E. SYRUPS Now it's time to stock your station with yumminess. You can easily order inexpensive coffee and tea syrups online, and feel like a full-fledged barista. Keeping them on a tray will make them handy to use and easy to move when you need extra counter space.

F. STIR SPOONS Find some wooden disposable stir sticks to keep on hand, or stock a stand or jar with washable spoons.

018 CREATE A HOMEMADE COCKTAIL BAR

Shake up a fabulous martini by creating your very own cocktail bar. By investing in a few essential tools, spirits, mixers, and glasses, you'll be able to jazz up your night with dozens of cocktails at your fingertips. It's not necessary to stock your bar with every kind of liquor available. A bottle of each of the basics and a few mixers will do just fine. Don't want to purchase everything all at once? Begin with ingredients from your favorite drinks and go from there.

TOOLS OF THE TRADE
- ☐ Recipe book
- ☐ Shaker, strainer, and jigger
- ☐ Ice bucket
- ☐ Stirring spoon and muddler

SPIRITS
- ☐ Vodka
- ☐ Tequila
- ☐ Rum
- ☐ Whiskey
- ☐ Cognac
- ☐ Gin
- ☐ Bourbon

MIXERS
- ☐ Cocktail liqueurs
- ☐ Bitters
- ☐ Dry and sweet vermouth
- ☐ Fruit juices
- ☐ Cocktail syrup
- ☐ Tabasco sauce
- ☐ Tonic water and soda
- ☐ Olive brine

OTHER ESSENTIALS
- ☐ Sugar cubes
- ☐ Cocktail skewers
- ☐ Citrus juicer
- ☐ Cutting board and knife

GLASSES (6 OF EACH)
Short (lowball), high (tallboy), stem glasses (wine, champagne, martini), and shot glasses

Use unexpected storage solutions and mixed materials to liven up a monochromatic kitchen.

019

FOCUS ON YOUR FRIDGE

A clean kitchen just isn't complete without giving your refrigerator a good once-over. It's easy, takes less than an hour, and looks fabulous once you're done!

STEP ONE Remove all drawers and shelves. Scrub them clean with mild soap and water and replace.

STEP TWO Place washable lining on the shelves and in the drawers. It's stylish and, most importantly, meant to absorb spills. Replace this lining about every six months.

STEP THREE Use organizing bins on the shelves. They're great for grouping like items, preventing leftovers from getting lost in the back, and keeping kids' school lunches and snacks handy.

STEP FOUR Gather your condiments together in one bin.

STEP FIVE Use containers inside the drawers to keep items like cheeses organized. When it's time to figure out what you need at the store, it only takes a quick glance to write down your shopping list.

020

MAKE LABELS YOUR FRIENDS

Take your fridge organization to a new level by labeling the containers. To encourage good habits, prepackage individual snack bags of fruits and veggies and watch how fast you'll begin reaching for the healthy snacks rather than the not-so-healthy ones. Try it—it really works!

021
MAKE SENSE OF YOUR FREEZER

The kitchen is much more efficient when everything is in its place and easily accessible. Having an organized freezer will save your family both time and money.

DIVIDE AND CONQUER Separate all your items into categories based on how often you use them.

USE A COLOR SYSTEM Implement colorful bins to group your items—as a bonus, it will also make the freezer more eye-catching.

COLLECT YOUR BINS Once you figure out how many categories you're dealing with, it's time to gather up your supplies. You will need at least one bin for each category. You can find inexpensive plastic bins just about anywhere these days.

LABEL CLEARLY If you want to be even more organized, you can label each bin with a food category. It might seem too obvious, but it will help other family members put food away correctly after grocery shopping.

STOCK UP! Now that your freezer is ready and waiting, it's time to stock up on groceries and kiss freezer burn goodbye (see item 022).

022
PREVENT FREEZER BURN

Freezer burn isn't inevitable—you can prevent it if you use your newly organized freezer to your advantage. The bins will maximize efficiency while meal planning (and during last-minute "what are we going to make for dinner?!" moments) and help prevent that frozen meat from languishing beneath a pile for weeks. Every month, sort through each bin so the oldest items get to be front and center. Go one step further and seal your food in food-saver bags.

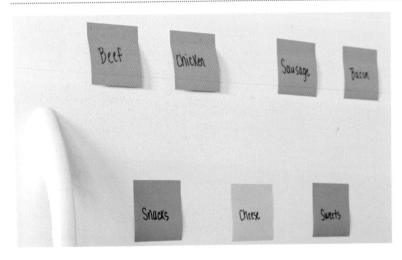

023 GO DEEP

If your family size or your wallet dictate that you buy in bulk, you've likely come across a pressing need for more storage. Deep freezers are a great solution, particularly when every item is made easy to find .

REMOVE AND SORT Pull everything out of the freezer and dispose of anything expired or freezer-burnt. Donate anything that's still good but you know your family won't use.

GO FOR A DEEP CLEAN These freezers are often overlooked. Take advantage of this time by cleaning the freezer inside and out.

SEPARATE AND CATEGORIZE Once you can see everything clearly, separate your items into categories. These will be unique to your family and might include meat, game meat, drinks, snacks, and sides.

USE DRAWER DIVIDERS Now that you're ready to put everything back, think about how to divide up the space. You can order fancy freezer dividers online, or be a bit more thrifty and make use of plastic reusable grocery bags.

LABEL THE SYSTEM Don't let your freezer go unused. Use sticky notes or another labeling system to keep tabs on what's inside—without having to dive through the icy depths to find out. This will also help other meal planners and helpers know where to find the good stuff. (Unless, of course, you want to be the only one in charge of where the cheesecake is kept!)

024
ASSESS THOSE APPLIANCES

Small appliances are fun to shop for—but after their initial use, most seem to disappear into the darkness of our cabinets. Follow these simple steps to take control of your small appliance collection.

TAKE INVENTORY
Before organizing your appliances, pull them all out of hiding and take inventory. How many do you have? Which appliances have collected dust? Which ones do you use most often? Can you live without any of them? So often we end up with things like panini presses or pasta machines that are fun at first, but just don't stand the test of time. You might also have multiple sizes of similar appliances.

CONSIDER THE USES Examine your applicances' multiple functions. If you have a blender that can act as a food processor, think about letting the food processor go.

CATEGORIZE Separate the appliances into two categories: "rarely use" and "use often." Only keep what you actually use and can't live without, and purge the rest. Maybe you only make popcorn with that air popper for an annual movie night blowout. It's not worth keeping just for that—microwave popcorn will do the trick. Or give it to a friend who's always loved it, and borrow it back once a year!

STOW AWAY Keep small appliances off the kitchen counter. Store them together in a kitchen cabinet or pantry. Out of sight means less visual clutter, but things hidden in the cabinet tend to be forgotten. So only store what you will use.

025
SORT BY FUNCTION

When storing your small appliances—the ones you really can't live without, remember?—it's best if you can group them by type. Otherwise, even in a relatively small kitchen, you're likely to end up forgetting what you have and where you put it. Note that for some people, some of the appliances below are on the "I would never use that" list. But for every fondue pot gathering dust in a cabinet somewhere, there's a family that just loves their melted cheese. (Still, just because it's on this list doesn't mean I'm giving you permission to keep it!)

MIX Group your stand mixer, hand mixer, food processor, blender, and juicer together in a cabinet or closet.

HEAT This category includes the toaster, toaster oven, panini press, popcorn machine, fondue maker, and waffle iron.

COOK Here's where you stash the rice cooker, slow cooker, bread machine, and deep fryer.

026
KEEP FAVORITE UTENSILS HANDY

I use wooden spoons and spatulas constantly for cooking and baking. I like them because they are durable and natural, and I keep them stored in an old crock on my counter. I also keep other favorites on hand, like metal whisks and spatulas. And since they're the ones I reach for most often, having them out on the counter makes sense for my kitchen. If you have a set of favorite stirrers or scrapers, try storing them in a cute flowerpot or vintage cookie jar to give your counter a little unexpected flair.

027
STOW POTS AND PANS

Pots and pans are an essential part of life, and most of us have a dedicated storage area for them (see item 011). Somehow, however, they always end up in precarious stacks, with the one thing you want inevitably at the very back of the cabinet. Here's how to take charge.

EVALUATE EVERYTHING Pull out every single pot and pan—including woks, roasting pans, stockpots, and frying pans. Really think about each item and decide how often you use it. If it's pretty but you never use it, put it in the donate pile. If

it's burnt, deeply scratched (in the case of nonstick pans), or made of aluminum, get rid of it. You only want healthy, high-quality pans in your home.

CONSIDER STORAGE You might want to look at replacing an under-stove cabinet with deep slide-out drawers. Stack pans as tidily as possible, grouping like with like. Also consider a mounted pot rack or pegboard system, and designate a shallower drawer for storing the lids.

028

GREEN UNDER YOUR KITCHEN SINK

Are you informed about the chemicals you are being exposed to? What's stopping you from switching to healthier options? Going green doesn't happen in a day, but there are many small changes you can incorporate that make a big difference, improving the overall health of your family and helping to prevent illnesses related to toxic and synthetic chemicals. Here are a few places to get started.

TRY BAKING SODA Anything that needs scrubbing can be cleaned with baking soda and elbow grease. It's cheap, natural, and works well.

USE ESSENTIAL OILS Swap out your cleaning products with synthetic fragrances for pure essential oils. Essential oils not only add a pleasant aroma while cleaning, but they clean effectively and deodorize naturally. Synthetic fragrances contain neurotoxins, phthalates, allergens, and sensitizers, all of which are harmful to your health.

BUY REUSABLE PRODUCTS To clean green, you should really eliminate—or at least lighten your use of—paper towels. Invest in some microfiber cloths and keep them handy under your kitchen sink. You can also find environmentally friendly gloves to take care of your beautiful hands. Make sure they are reusable, and enjoy saving the planet.

LOOK FOR NONTOXIC DISH DETERGENTS AND CLEANERS There are many methods for washing dishes the green way. For those with the option, it's more eco-friendly to wash your dishes in the dishwasher, since it uses less water than washing them by hand. Also be sure to avoid synthetic dyes and fragrances, and choose phosphate-free soaps.

029

CLEAN YOUR OVEN WITH BAKING SODA

Cleaning your oven with traditional oven cleaners is one of the most toxic things you can do in your home. If you're like most families, your oven is probably covered in a couple years' worth of baking grime. The good news is that with a little elbow grease and baking soda, toxic products are unnecessary.

STEP ONE Vacuum out crumbs and loose debris.

STEP TWO Coat the oven entirely with baking soda. Obviously, make sure the oven is completely cool to the touch before you do this.

STEP THREE Using a spray bottle, mist the baking soda with water until it becomes damp. The mixture of baking soda and water will break down grease and grime. Use a sponge to spread the mixture throughout the entire oven.

STEP FOUR Over the next couple of hours, continue spraying the baking soda as it dries, keeping it moist.

STEP FIVE Scrape out the baking soda, taking grease and food particles along for the ride.

STEP SIX Using a sponge and the spray bottle, thoroughly rinse the oven. You're done!

A stove hood does a lot to keep a kitchen grime-free. Make sure to return the favor by wiping it down regularly!

Utilize vertical storage by installing cabinets that reach all the way to the ceiling.

030
ORGANIZE UNDER THE SINK

Space tends to be at a premium under the kitchen sink (especially if you have a garbage disposal, or your dishwasher pipes run through the space), so make sure you use every last bit of available room to store your cleaning supplies. I love my organized cabinet, but it wasn't always so neat. At one time, junk would literally fall out every time I opened the door. No longer! Here's how to take control.

ACCESSORIZE Before you sort and clean, take a look at how the empty space is organized. I bet you can get a lot more out of it with a few reasonably priced accessories. I have built-in door racks, but you can get the same convenience with wire racks that hook over the cabinet doors. Think about what kinds of stacking bins and trays will be useful. One product I love is

3M's Command hooks. They stick on, so you don't have to go to the trouble of drilling holes, and they are surprisingly sturdy. I use them to hang dishwashing gloves, a scrub brush, a squeegee, a lint roller, and other things I want to lay my hands on easily throughout the day.

SORT AND PURGE Once you've got your supplies, it's time to clear the clutter. Take everything out of the cabinet and sort by category (sponges and cloths, dish soap,

household cleaners, that sort of thing). Throw away anything you never use, including any spare spray bottles and containers with a tiny bit of product in the bottom. Consider replacing your toxic cleaners with all-natural ones (see item 028). If you do discard anything toxic, consult your local waste management service to find out how to safely dispose of it.

CLEAN UP Spray and wipe down the area really well and, when dry, put down some contact paper. If you're using the Command hooks, note that they need to set for an hour before you hang anything on them.

GET ORGANIZED Put your supplies into the bins and baskets you've prepared, and put them back in an orderly fashion. I have a metal organizer for my candles, and plastic bins for scrubbing brushes, microfiber cloths, and hand soap. Place dishwasher pods or liquids in a sealed tub. I keep my dish rack under the sink, as well, ready to be used when needed.

031
MAKE THAT SINK SPARKLE

At this point we've cleaned and organized everything but the kitchen sink. What's next? You guessed it! It's a battle for me to keep the sink clean on a daily basis, but an easy cleaner helps (see item 004). One thing that I find very effective is my weekly routine. It's simple but it works. Just follow these steps to a happier sink.

STEP ONE Rinse the dirty sink out really well, with no remaining food particles or gunk.

STEP TWO Apply a cleaning paste like Shaklee Scour Off, using lots of elbow grease. Paste works better

than most powdered cleaners, as it doesn't make big dust clouds and it adheres well to those vertical sink walls. If you don't have Scour Off, whip up a homemade cleansing paste using ½ cup baking soda, a teaspoon of Castile soap, and enough water to make a paste.

STEP THREE Scrub everything really well, then rinse off thoroughly.

STEP FOUR Spray the sink with a natural cleaning spray, then rinse again. Lastly, wipe down with a soft towel. Admire your handiwork and enjoy that sparkling sink!

032
TAME THE JUNK DRAWER

A junk drawer can be found in virtually every kitchen across the world. Its sole purpose is to contain items you have no designated spot for, so it's no wonder it gets out of hand in a hurry. Take a few minutes to go through your junk drawer and purge anything you haven't used in a while, or anything that doesn't serve a purpose. You'll find that most of the items can be eliminated. Who needs a lone screw you will never use or ten random Allen wrenches?

Once you finish purging, remove the rest of the junk and wipe out the drawer. Then grab a few organizers (you can recycle cardboard jewelry boxes or sturdy plastic containers that you may have been saving—possibly even in that junk drawer!) and categorize your miscellaneous items. By removing clutter and purging the things that are no longer useful, you can control the junk and maintain organization. Allow yourself a few minutes each month to go through the drawer and tidy it.

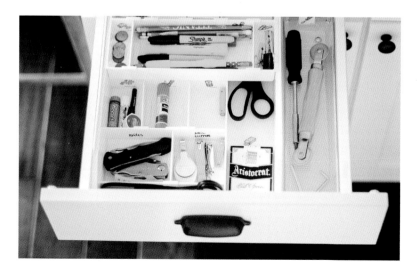

033

MAXIMIZE STORAGE IN A TINY KITCHEN

Every bit of space counts in a small kitchen, so look at every wall and surface and strategize about ways to utilize it. Whether you're a renter, a condo dweller, or part of the tiny-house trend, here are a few ideas to consider as you look to get the most out of a cute, cozy space.

SHELVE IT Consider every possible place where you can add shelving for pantry essentials. If the containers are attractive enough, your essentials can be on display without feeling like clutter. Just don't let the shelves get messy or dusty. In addition, risers or additional shelves inside your cabinets are a great solution for smaller items, like canned goods, that can stack two or three levels deep. And racks that fit over cabinet doors are a great way to store spices, tea, and other small items on the inside of the doors.

HANG OUT Hanging baskets can be used to store fruit, garlic, and other items that would otherwise be taking up counter space.

SNEAK IN STORAGE Spots that are often used exclusively for decoration can actually become handy storage. The false drawer under most sinks can be replaced with a tilt-out drawer front that's great for storing sponges and scrub pads. Even more crafty, Ikea has a cupboard solution that sneaks a drawer into the bottom-of-the-cabinet toekick space. Nobody will suspect that's where your muffin tins are hiding!

MAKE A PANTRY If you don't have a pantry, consider buying a standing cabinet (you can probably find a vintage wardrobe or even a dresser with deep drawers and refinish or paint it to suit). You can place it where it's convenient, and free up your cabinets for other things.

034

ADD SURFACES

One of the main complaints about smaller kitchens is the lack of workspace. Once you've implemented some of the storage solutions in item 33, your surfaces will be less cluttered, but there's still only so much counter space available in a small room. Here are a few ways to eke out a bit more.

ADD ISLANDS You likely won't be installing a real kitchen island in your tiny space, but a rolling table or cart allows you to add another work surface and, as a bonus, can give you several tiers of built-in storage.

SLIDE OUT A lot of kitchens have cutting boards that slide out from under the counter and then stow away when no longer needed. If your kitchen doesn't have any, look into having them installed. It might be well worth it.

FOLD DOWN Many of us have heard tales of Depression-era relatives eating dinner off of fold-down ironing boards. The more workable version of this is a fold-out kitchen table. It becomes a great option for adding a work surface or small dining space as needed.

KEEP IT CLEAN Ask anyone with a small kitchen—the number-one method for maximizing space is preventing clutter. In a bigger kitchen, a stack of dishes on the counter is unsightly, but it doesn't render the kitchen unusable. In a cramped space, those dishes may be taking up your entire available prep area. Clean and purge as you go, always, in order to keep your space user-friendly.

036
GO VERTICAL

No matter how small the footprint of your kitchen is, there's probably wall and shelf space going unused. Take a look at these solutions and start looking up. And down.

- ☐ Hang pots and pans overhead, and consider mounting a sheet of pegboard for utensils.

- ☐ Consider installing a small microwave on the wall or in a cabinet to free up counter space.

- ☐ Hanging mugs from hooks along the bottom of a shelf frees up space and looks fun and cozy.

- ☐ Attach small jars to the undersides of shelves and cabinets—you can just unscrew them when you need the spice or tea within, then screw them back on.

- ☐ A magnetic knife strip on the wall can make an otherwise blank space very handy.

- ☐ Squeeze tall, skinny shelving units into any space you can. Even if the shelves that fit between your fridge and the wall can only hold a few cookbooks, those are cookbooks that aren't taking up space anywhere else!

- ☐ Speaking of the fridge, place baskets or even risers on top of it to expand the space there.

- ☐ If there's space between your top cabinets and the ceilings, baskets and bins up there can hold rarely used items.

035
WASTE NOT

One big challenge in a small kitchen is waste disposal, especially if you live in an area where you need to separate landfill trash, recycling, and compost. There's hardly space for one bin, never mind three separate receptacles, and who wants to be navigating around them and having to look at them all day, anyway?

One great solution is a slide-out under-sink sorting system. You can find these bin systems at home improvement stores for under $100 USD, and they're pretty easy to install. They essentially consist of a metal rack and two to four sorting bins. You screw the metal rack into your under-sink cabinet, then mount the bins on the rack, and you can then slide each bin in and out as needed. As a bonus, the system keeps pets or toddlers from monkeying with the trash.

WEEK 1
THE KITCHEN
Challenge

THE KITCHEN IS THE HUB OF the home. Everyone ends up in there at some point during their day, so it gets messy—and the mess happens fast! The best way to conquer the clutter is to get organized. Before using all of the kitchen tips and tools in this book, begin the process by clearing out the space and starting from scratch. Over the next seven days, you'll be rejuvenating your kitchen and, hopefully, falling in love with it again, so allocate your time well. Don't tear everything apart if you won't be able to get it back together in a week. Take note that we're not tackling the pantry this week—that'll come next.

To get fully organized, you want to get as much of a fresh start as possible. That means emptying out every cabinet and drawer in your kitchen. Get a babysitter, put on your comfy clothes, and turn up the music. It's time to organize!

THE PROCESS

1. PREPARE
Clear off the kitchen table. This is going to be your dumping grounds and staging area for the rest of the process.

2. SORT AND PURGE
Empty the contents of all the cabinets and drawers onto the table, as well as everything from the kitchen counters and the under-sink cabinet. Organize all items by category. (Everyone's categories will be a little bit different, so figure out what works for you.) Discard old, expired, and no longer used items. Check the dates. Place everything you can into bins, baskets, and drawer organizers, by category.

3. CLEAN
Now it's time to clean that kitchen! Wipe down the counters and the backsplash with a good natural cleaner, and clean countertops and tables. Reline the drawers and shelves if necessary. Wipe down all appliances, large and small, mop the floors, and wipe down the table and chairs.

4. ORGANIZE
Put the items you use on a daily basis back on the countertop, and place your bins and organizers back into cabinets and drawers, sorted by category of item. Moving forward, keep all clutter off the counters at all times. If you take it out, put it away!

5. FREE UP THE FRIDGE
Finally, take everything out of the fridge and freezer, and place it on the table. Toss anything that you never use, and frozen food that you're never going to eat. Wipe the fridge and freezer out, and put everything back in an organized manner. Take everything off the refrigerator door, as a cluttered surface makes the kitchen look messy.

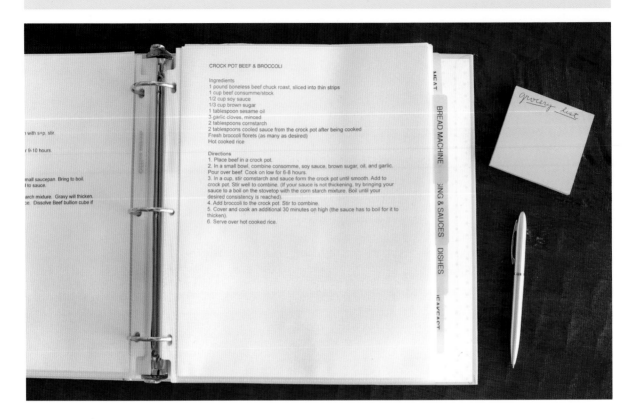

Within the cropped image, the recipe reads:

CROCK POT BEEF & BROCCOLI

Ingredients
1 pound boneless beef chuck roast, sliced into thin strips
1 cup beef consomme/stock
1/2 cup soy sauce
1/3 cup brown sugar
1 tablespoon sesame oil
3 garlic cloves, minced
2 tablespoons cornstarch
2 tablespoons cooled sauce from the crock pot after being cooked
Fresh broccoli florets (as many as desired)
Hot cooked rice

Directions
1. Place beef in a crock pot.
2. In a small bowl, combine consomme, soy sauce, brown sugar, oil, and garlic. Pour over beef. Cook on low for 6-8 hours.
3. In a cup, stir cornstarch and sauce form the crock pot until smooth. Add to crock pot. Stir well to combine. (If your sauce is not thickening, try bringing your sauce to a boil on the stovetop with the corn starch mixture. Boil until your desired consistency is reached.)
4. Add broccoli to the crock pot. Stir to combine.
5. Cover and cook an additional 30 minutes on high (the sauce has to boil for it to thicken).
6. Serve over hot cooked rice.

037
CREATE A RECIPE BINDER

With the Internet at our fingertips these days, people are using cookbooks much less than they once did. In the blink of an eye, we can simply print out a recipe, and, if it was a hit, file it to use another day. Our family's recipe binder is filled with meals that we've loved for years. It's become an heirloom piece, full of recipes that we've raised our children with and will be enjoyed for years to come.

Here's how you can create your own recipe binder in about 30 minutes.

YOU'LL NEED

☐ Academic binder
☐ Printer and paper
☐ Page protectors
☐ Tabs
☐ Labels
☐ Pencil pouch for small recipe cards

CATEGORIZE Create category tabs using adhesive office tabs, a label maker, or your computer. Print the tabs out on cardstock, then cut to size. Categories may include:

☐ Appetizers
☐ Bread
☐ Soup
☐ Salad
☐ Meat
☐ Vegetarian
☐ Slow Cooker
☐ Breakfast
☐ Dessert
☐ Pasta
☐ Casseroles
☐ Holidays
☐ Grilling
☐ Juices/Smoothies

ASSEMBLE THE BINDER Place about ten page protectors between each category divider. Collect your favorite recipes and slide them in.

FINISH UP Design a cover and place it in the front of the binder. Add your family name for a special touch.

038 BIN YOUR CANS

Organizing canned goods was quite difficult for me to figure out. We don't go through a huge amount of canned food, but there are certain staples that I use on a regular basis, like canned tomatoes and beans. I didn't want the cans to take up a lot of room in the pantry, so I found some plastic storage bins online. They were inexpensive and the perfect size for the job—the larger for medium and large cans, and the smaller bin for tomato paste and diced pepper cans.

039 STORE MEDICINE AND VITAMINS PROPERLY

Proper medication and vitamin storage is very important, and most of us are doing it completely wrong. When storing medication and vitamins, be sure to keep them away from extreme temperatures—hot or cold. Don't store them in the bathroom medicine cabinet—it's actually the worst place, due to temperature and moisture. A kitchen cabinet away from the oven is good.

LABEL Gather several containers and label each by category.

- ☐ Children's medications
- ☐ Fever and pain
- ☐ First aid (bandages, ointment, wound cleanser)
- ☐ Splints and wraps
- ☐ Eyes, ears, nose, skin
- ☐ Allergy and bug bites
- ☐ Bowels and belly
- ☐ Vitamins
- ☐ Prescription medicine

PURGE Check all expiration dates and purge expired items before organizing them into the containers.

STORE Leave vitamins and medicine in their original containers. Some supplements lose their effectiveness when exposed to light, for example, which is the reason for their dark-colored plastic containers. Avoid combining your vitamins with other supplements.

CHECK Before you flush expired products down the toilet, look them up on the FDA website to learn how to dispose of them properly.

040 USE THE "ONE-DOOR"

Many kitchens have at least one odd cabinet out, especially in rooms that aren't perfect squares or rectangles. A kitchen in a historic home might be built around servants' quarters and dumbwaiters, and could have some odd angles and leftover cabinet space where a pair of facing cabinets won't fit. Even modern kitchens usually have a few single-door cabinet spaces, and they're perfect for storing medications and non-food substances you want the whole family to be aware—and careful—of.

Teach your kids that the "one-door" isn't for snacks, but contains medicine and other grown-up items. Make sure it's part of an upper cabinet (out of very small children's reach) and that it's far enough from the oven to avoid heating up your meds (see item 039, left). The whole family will know where to find the things that don't quite fit in with the rest of the kitchen.

041

ORGANIZE YOUR PANTRY

I'm constantly working on organization systems within my home, especially if they are magnet areas for clutter like the pantry. I know the system isn't working if I've organized a space and suddenly, two days later, it's a mess again.

That's what happened with my pantry, so I tried out a few different systems until I found what worked for us. Using a few containers, baskets, and bins, you can break down your pantry organization into categories and make the space work better for you. You can see how the organizers at Neat Method reworked this pantry at right.

Start by categorizing the space and the items going into it. Chances are, you've got a lot of food taking up a lot of space. Using these groupings really helped sort out this magnet-for-madness area in my home.

BASIC PANTRY CATEGORIES

- ☐ Baking supplies (this is for cases in which you don't have or need a baking station)
- ☐ Bulk items (rice, beans, nuts, and other bulk dry goods)
- ☐ Canned food
- ☐ Pasta and pasta sauces
- ☐ Chocolate and desserts
- ☐ Prepackaged food
- ☐ Snacks

042 CONTROL YOUR CANNED GOODS

Another option for corralling the various cans of soup, sauces, fruits, veggies, and other shelf-stable items is to utilize wall-mounted wire baskets—or an over-the-door organizer (see item 043). These racks are often found in the closet storage sections of stores, rather than intended for pantry use, but some are perfectly sized for holding a rack of cans—and they're nice and sturdy, so they can support the heavy weight of all those cans.

043

USE YOUR DOORS

You don't want to forget to use the valuable space on the inside of your pantry doors. Door organizers can be found at most home stores or online. They work great for storing bottles of food, sauces, and frequently used canned goods.

044 START WITH AN INVENTORY

When you organize your pantry, keep track of what you have by using a pantry inventory sheet. I keep my sheets on a clipboard, hanging on the wall inside my pantry. With these sheets, grocery shopping will be a breeze.

045

THINK ABOUT STORAGE

There are several methods for organizing food in your pantry, including clear containers, baskets, and plastic bins. I mix it up and use all of the above.

CLEAR POP-TOP CONTAINERS
Clear containers, like my favorite set from OXO, are excellent for storing pasta, grains, and rice. Once I get home from grocery shopping, I empty all the pasta boxes and place everything in these containers. Cardboard food boxes clutter the space, so using clear containers has helped us stay more organized.

BASKETS Woven baskets are effective organizers for the pantry when you use them correctly—but I don't recommend them for everything. They're nice to look at,

but the large sizes can become so full of food that you can't see what's at the bottom. However, baskets work well to store items like bags of food, snacks, prepackaged breakfast items, large quantities of the same item, and extra canned goods.

PLASTIC BINS Colorful bins are great for storing reusable food containers and their lids. You can use different colors to separate categories and make daily organizing a breeze.

From Toni

Becky Barnfather will motivate and inspire you to give your home the attention it needs at organizingmadefun.com.

BECKY, **ORGANIZING MADE FUN**

66 When we first moved into our current home, I was thrilled to have a small walk-in pantry. The previous owner had used it solely as a place for storing dishes and it wasn't well set up for organization, so it got messy easily. Through the years, I attempted to organize it and to keep things in it looking nice, but no matter how organized I had it, it seemed that it was still hard to tell when I was running out of food and it still looked haphazard because the rest of the family really didn't put things back in the spots I'd designated.

Finally, I purchased large mason jars, clear containers, and white bins from Ikea and Target. I tried to find containers for each dry good that could hold all of what comes in each box or bag so that I didn't have extra contents to deal with or store separately. Now I can look into the pantry and see exactly what is left in each container. And, with simple chalkboard labels that are easy to change, everyone puts things back where they belong.

I also added a bold, patterned wallpaper to give it a pop when you open the pantry door. All the black and white inside helps to keep it looking clean and neat—even if it's not perfect—and allows the food to show through easily in the clear jars. 99

BEFORE

046
PACK YOUR SNACKS

Whether you're heading to the office, going to the park with your kids, or planning to run errands all day, you don't want to find yourself empty-handed in the snack department. To avoid those nasty hunger pangs, it's all about implementing a plan of attack.

THINK HEALTHY Healthy snacks can boost your metabolism and help fight the urge to overeat during regular mealtime. As you get ready to do your weekly grocery shopping, plan to purchase healthy snack options for yourself and your family. Select a variety of items that you will look forward to munching on, and make them easy to access in your kitchen setup.

PLAN AHEAD Set aside some time each week to section out and pack up your munchies. Use reusable containers to store and organize your snacks. Get all of the prep work done at one time. When washed and ready-to-go single servings are available, you'll save fruits and veggies from rotting in the fridge or on the counter before anyone remembers to eat them. Plus, when your appetite calls, you'll have a quick answer!

STASH YOUR NIBBLES The key to having healthy snacks when you need them is to have them *where* you need them. Stash some in your car, purse, desk drawer, fridge, and any other place where you might need to have quick access for a snack attack!

THINK OUTSIDE THE BOX Be creative with your snack options by adding variety, interest, and even a little something sweet. A square of dark chocolate on a chilly afternoon with some hot tea is a lovely, decadent option—and it won't ruin your appetite like a bag of chips and a soda would.

KEEP A LIST OF SNACK IDEAS Snacks don't have to come in flashy packages to be satisfying. Remember these options:

- ☐ Nuts (all kinds)
- ☐ Dried fruit
- ☐ Fresh fruit or veggies and dips
- ☐ Yogurt or cheese
- ☐ Dark chocolate
- ☐ Air-popped popcorn
- ☐ Healthy crackers or chips
- ☐ Granola or protein bars

047
CREATE A SCHOOL LUNCH STATION

Making school lunches can be a headache when all the components are scattered in different places around the kitchen. Designating a special place for everything you need not only makes your morning routine run more smoothly—it also allows your children to help out.

STEP ONE Designate a drawer or shelf with enough room to store everything you'll need. Keep a small cutting board handy for sandwiches.

STEP TWO Use smaller containers to separate items like snack and sandwich bags, utensils, tinfoil, Tupperware, and other building blocks.. Don't forget napkins and moist wipes.

STEP THREE Replace hard lunch boxes with softer cloth bags (the insulated kinds are perfect) for more compact storage.

048

PLAN MEALS IN ADVANCE

You know the familiar question before it's even asked: "What's for dinner?" To avoid running on empty or being forced to pick fast food over healthier options, a little advance planning will go a long way.

STEP ONE Choose one night a week for menu planning. It's fun to get the kids involved. Remember to look at their school lunch schedule, if you have one, to add to or complement the meals they are already eating.

STEP TWO Look over your family's schedule so you know when everyone is home, which days you are going to need a quick dinner, and which days you'll be able to linger over a meal.

STEP THREE Be realistic with your time. Most weeknights you will want a nutritious yet quick dinner, while on weekends you can prep the slow cooker, let the tomato sauce simmer, or designate family BBQ time.

STEP FOUR Build your dinners around your fussiest eaters. It's not necessary to cook something new every single time you're in the kitchen. Establish a bank of twenty or so recipes and switch them around. Work in a new one here and there (see step six).

STEP FIVE Focus on the main dish and build your sides around it, then make use of the leftovers! An uneaten side of corn one night can become a tasty layer in shepherd's pie the next.

STEP SIX Try a new recipe at least once a month. This will open up your options and introduce your family members (even the picky ones!) to new experiences. You might wind up with a new go-to in the rotation.

STEP SEVEN Browse the coupon section of your local paper and use the specials to inspire you.

STEP EIGHT Take stock of what you already have in your pantry and which items need to be used up soon, then plan your menu to incorporate them.

049

SHOP EFFECTIVELY

Getting organized will carry over to all parts of your life. You might think a trip to the grocery store will be the same every time, but with an organized shopping list, it's faster and easier than ever before. If you have a regular weekly food shopping routine, step it up a notch by prepping your shopping list based on your kitchen inventory. Here's how to make this chore a breeze.

KEEP A LIST Start with a master list—all the time. These are the items you need to replenish every week without fail. Store this on your computer, print out several copies to keep in the kitchen, and add to it as needed.

MAKE SPACE Clear out the fridge and food storage areas to get rid of any too-old leftovers and make room for new purchases. Take stock of your pantry and decide which items you'd like to purchase.

FINALIZE THE LIST Consult your weekly menu and add any new items you know you need.

UPDATE YOUR STOCK Check off items as you buy them. If there is a staple on the list that you don't need this week, cross it out.

HAVE A BULK LIST Keep a separate list for items you regularly buy in bulk, like paper products, frozen goods, and vitamins.

THAW OUT!

For easy reheating, transfer your frozen foods from the freezer to the refrigerator the night before, then bake in the oven. Add about 10 to 15 minutes if the center is still frozen.

Your best oils and vinegars are for special meals, so they don't need to be stored with your commonly used condiments.

050

LIVEN UP YOUR MENU WITH A THEME NIGHT

Theme menus spice up your evening and allow your family the chance to explore new flavors and learn about different cultures. On a special night, take the experience even further with theme music and décor.

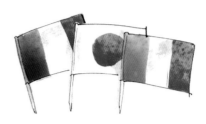

THEME	MENU	BEVERAGES	FLAIR
Italian	Caprese salad (tomato, basil, fresh mozzarella cheese), a pasta course like spaghetti with meatballs, and tiramisu for dessert.	Red table wine. Negronis, or prosecco.	Turn on *The Godfather* soundtrack or Italian opera music.
Japanese	Miso soup, edamame with fresh garlic, tuna maki, and teriyaki chicken with rice. Have some green tea ice cream for dessert.	Sake, green tea, or Japanese beer.	Move cushions to your living room floor and eat around your coffee table.
Mexican	Taco night with a mix of ground beef, shredded chicken, and a variety of toppings, plus flan for dessert.	Mexican beer or margaritas.	Listen to Latin jazz or Mexican mariachi music in the background.
Southern BBQ	Pork ribs and grilled chicken with cornbread, black-eyed peas, and peach cobbler for dessert.	Old-fashioned lemonade or iced tea.	Eat outside with gingham napkins and tablecloths.
French	Frisée salad topped with fried lardon and a poached egg, ginger and carrot soup served with crusty bread, and fresh sorbet for dessert.	Chilled, French white wine.	Edith Piaf's "La Vie en Rose."
Spanish Tapas	Green olives and manchego cheese, paella (any recipe you prefer), and coconut ice cream for dessert.	Muddled rum drinks with sprigs of mint.	Serve meals on tiny side plates for a tapas experience.

051

UTILIZE YOUR FREEZER

For those of you on the go, especially if you have kids at home, your mantra should be, "Make the freezer your friend." Soups, side dishes, and desserts can easily be made in bulk and then stored in the freezer until you're ready to eat.

SOUPS Make stocks or soups up to two weeks in advance and store them in 2-cup (0.5-liter) increments for easy, single-serve defrosting.

BAKED GOODS Stock your freezer with muffins, pancakes, biscuits, scones, waffles, and other baked goods, which can be frozen and toasted up for a hot, buttery morning treat.

LEFTOVERS Double your recipes and store leftovers in individual packets so that you just have to throw them in the microwave for a quick, easy meal.

WEEK 2
THE PANTRY
Challenge

We conquered the entire kitchen last week, and this week we are going to roll up our sleeves to clean out and organize the pantry. This week will be a lighter workload; after all that work in the kitchen, you deserve a break!

You also deserve an organized pantry, and the steps to the right will get you just that. Of course, every family's pantry is different, so customize the steps to suit your needs. If you don't have a dedicated pantry per se, use the same tips to organize whatever food cabinets or shelves you do have.

THE PROCESS

1. PLAN
Before you start, make sure you have a good supply of boxes, bins, and airtight food containers (I like the OXO line). You will find these really helpful, but if you don't have any and want to get started, you can just organize your food into categories on the kitchen table.

2. SET UP
Line up your empty bins, baskets, and containers on the kitchen table, or clear off the surface to make room for new stacks.

3. PURGE
Take everything out of your pantry. Check the expiration dates and throw out expired items, as well as any open packages of things that you never use, whether they're expired or not. Items that you will never use that are still sealed can be set aside for donation to a local food pantry.

4. ORGANIZE
Place like items in the baskets on the table (or, if you're not using baskets, sort them by category). Organizing your food into categories in bins will help keep your pantry looking nice and neat. Your categories will be specific to your family, but consider including: school, breakfast, pasta, baking, sauce, bread, snacks, sides, and so on. You can also empty bags and boxes of dry goods into clear canisters or mason jars.

5. CLEAN
Once you are finished organizing everything into categories, wipe out your pantry, then sweep and mop the floor. You want it to be nice and clean before you put everything away.

6. LABEL
Label each bin and container with a labeler, or hang a tag on the baskets or bins, or on the front of the shelves where they'll live.

7. TIDY
Place all of your neatly organized bins, boxes, and containers in their designated spots. Enjoy your newly efficient and organized pantry!

052
DESIGN YOUR DINING ROOM

The dining room is the space where we entertain our guests. It's also an area that shows our true personal style. Whether it's classic, contemporary, or vintage, choosing the right décor and pieces to fill the space will make it feel more authentic. There are six main concepts to consider when designing your dining room.

A. TABLE The center of the room is the dining table. Make sure the table is the correct size to fit the room. If you have a small room, you will want a smaller table when you're not entertaining, but you can add a leaf in the middle to accommodate more guests for meals or buffets.

B. CHAIRS How many chairs do you have? Depending on the size of your family, at least six chairs at the table and two extras placed to the side should suffice. When you're not entertaining, you can put a chair on either side of the hutch. Chairs don't necessarily have to match the table. Think outside of the box—you might like a white table and dark chairs, or mismatched antique chairs for an eclectic look.

C. WALL DÉCOR Fill the walls with décor that matches your style. An old, chipped window frame with a boxwood leaf wreath hanging from it is a great vintage touch, while a gallery wall filled with framed memories or an antique painting might suit a more classic style.

D. WINDOW TREATMENTS Blinds, curtains, drapes, or nothing at all—which will it be? Tailor your windows to fit your needs, but make sure to measure before you shop. If you're going to hang curtains, the higher up you hang the rods, the taller the ceilings and windows will appear to be. You can make a small window look much bigger by "cheating" the curtains so that they actually hang over the surrounding wall space.

E. CENTERPIECE A centerpiece warms the room and is a nice way to show off some details. Add a fresh flower arrangement to a beautiful vase, or fill a large porcelain bowl with fresh fruit. You can also lay a runner down the center for a more polished look. This is a great spot to show off your creativity!

F. BUFFET If you entertain a lot, I recommend adding a buffet in your dining room. This is where you place food for dinner parties or holiday celebrations. You can also use it to store liquor, wine, and cocktail glasses (see item 018).

053
SHOWCASE YOUR COLLECTIBLES

One of the most cherished pieces I have in my home is a vintage pie cabinet, containing all of my Jadeite dishes. I've been collecting Jadeite for about 15 years, and I've found pieces at antique stores, garage sales, thrift stores, and online using Ebay or Etsy. Whatever it is that you collect, display it proudly in a cabinet or on a shelf. I suggest placing the same type of collectibles or décor near each other. Things display more beautifully as a collection, rather than spread throughout your home. If your collectibles are breakable, make sure your cabinets have doors!

Quick Tip

STAY FOCUSED

Keep your dining room hutch exclusively for dining and entertainment storage. Remove all other items that belong elsewhere.

054
EMPLOY A DINING HUTCH

When it comes to organizing the dining room, furniture that comes with a good amount of storage is key, especially if you like to entertain. Using a dining hutch with shelving, drawers, and cabinets is the perfect way to contain this space, and you can find pieces of furniture in many styles and sizes. You can use drawers to hide smaller items and glass front cabinets to display your favorite pieces. Here are a few ways to divvy up your storage options:

CABINETS
- ☐ Seasonal table décor
- ☐ Holiday dishes
- ☐ Serving trays and bowls

SHELVES
- ☐ China
- ☐ Cake stands
- ☐ Picture frames or décor
- ☐ Vintage dishes

DRAWERS
- ☐ Napkin rings
- ☐ Cloth napkins
- ☐ Placemats
- ☐ Chargers
- ☐ Tablecloths and runners
- ☐ Extra silverware
- ☐ Placecards or frames
- ☐ Candles and lighter or matches

055

TABLE THE DISCUSSION

A dining table often feels like a luxury in a small apartment—and sometimes a true impossibility, depending on how tiny your space is. Here are a number of ways to work around that issue to create a dedicated dining area.

CIRCLE UP A compact, round table usually seats more people than a rectangular one, has a smaller footprint, and can be easily moved into a corner to make more floor space when needed.

DOUBLE UP It's OK to double-dip on how a space is used. A nice bar or counter can also be a cute diner-style eating surface for two. One hint: choose your barstools well. Without a footrest, you might end up feeling like your legs are asleep halfway through dinner.

KNOW WHEN TO FOLD 'EM Some folding tables are surprisingly chic, so don't discount this option without shopping around a bit. You can also look into tables that fold down from the wall, Murphy bed–style. You can also install a slide-out table under a counter, which you can eat on or use as an extra serving surface at parties.

TURN OVER A LEAF Tables with insertable leaves can be a great option if you have guests over a lot—just be sure you have a good spot to stash the leaves when they're not in use. Drop-leaf tables are another option, offering up extra table space in a jiffy.

GET A LEG UP If you have a space to store the pieces when not in use, a tabletop with screw-in legs can assemble easily, and the end result can be quite stylish.

056

DEFINE THE SPACE

To help define a small dining space, lighting can make a huge difference. Try hanging a pendant lamp over the table—especially if the table's not in a designated dining room. This really helps set the space apart from the rest of the room. If you rent or can't hang a light for other reasons, a nice lamp placed high behind the table is an alternate solution.

Another way to create a space within a space is to hang something on the wall that draws the eye upward and visually anchors the table. It might be a big mirror, a framed piece of art, or a funky wall clock. Experiment with what works in your home.

057
THROW A DINNER PARTY IN A SMALL SPACE

Having a tiny house or even living in a studio apartment shouldn't stop you from throwing a fun dinner party—whether or not you have a dining room, or even a dining room table. Your friends know you have a small space, and they won't be expecting a *Downton Abbey*–style dinner layout. So if you love to entertain, don't let a small space hold you back! Here are some hints to make it a snap.

MAKE ROOM Create a space for the party. This may mean rearranging furniture, or even stashing some pieces out of sight (like hiding a coffee table or a big armchair in the bedroom). A living room with the furniture moved out of the way can make a fine dining room for the space-challenged.

SET THE MOOD Low light and candles can focus the attention on the party area rather than highlighting the accommodations you've made to clear the space. A boldly colored bouquet can make a nice centerpiece that doesn't take up too much space on a small table.

SIT PRETTY If you often have people over, invest in some nice folding chairs that can be easily stashed. Or get really creative and have a Middle Eastern– or Japanese-themed dinner where guests can sit on pillows.

MIX IT UP If you really can't make a table and chairs work in your space or with your furniture, throw a cocktail party with appetizers placed around the room, instead. That way, if some folks sit and some stand, it won't feel awkward, and no one's balancing a full plate on their lap. Make the serving surfaces feel special with nice coverings (one idea: use mix-and-match cloth napkins, or coordinated fabric remnants cut to fit). With this kind of shindig, bookcases, end tables, and workspaces can be pressed into service as fine plate rests.

From Toni

Maria Gonzales is full of brilliant organizing ideas you'd never think of, and is the super-talented creator of the website gracefulorder.com.

MARIA, GRACEFUL ORDER

" As much as I preach about paring down and getting rid of excess, I love to be a prepared hostess. Over the years, I have collected pieces that I love and use for entertaining, and I have to admit that my dining room was in need of a little order.

My collection of napkins, napkin rings, place cards, and serving pieces didn't have a designated spot. What's worse, since nothing had a home, I started adding items to the drawer that had nothing to do with entertaining, like pens, paper, and random cards. The problem was that when I needed to set up for a party, I had to dig through a messy drawer to find what I needed. Sometimes I would forget I owned a piece because it simply wasn't visible.

I needed to start from scratch and reclaim my dining hutch. I already had the space, I just had to utilize it properly. After clearing out the drawers, sorting the many items, and finally organizing everything, I can say that I am definitely ready for my next dinner party! "

BEFORE

AFTER

058
THROW A CASUAL PARTY

Good organization is the key to any party. If you're planning to have folks over for a backyard barbecue or buffet supper, a few simple considerations can make the whole thing run more smoothly.

THINK ABOUT SPACE You may have a nice yard, but what if it unexpectedly rains or the wind kicks up? Everyone might end up clustered inside in a too-small living room. Don't invite more people than your home can comfortably hold, even if more could be happy in the yard. Of course, if you live somewhere with predictable weather, you can be more flexible. And remember: no matter what you do, partygoers will always flock to the kitchen.

CLEAR YOUR FRIDGE Let your basic stocks run a little low before the gathering so that you have extra space to stash the party food. If need be, bring out some camping coolers. Fill them with ice, and use them to keep things chilled.

DON'T OVERBUY Remember, not everyone is going to eat everything, and it's OK if grandma's special potato salad runs out before everyone gets to try it—as long as there are enough other dishes to go around. Bread and cheese can fill in a lot of gaps, and they're easy to use up or freeze if there are leftovers.

PLAN THE FLOW There's a reason cruise ship and fancy hotel buffets are set up the way they are. Learn from these experts, and create a natural flow for your guests. A stack of plates at one end of the table signifies that it's the starting point. It would seem logical to place the cutlery there, as well, but trying to juggle a plate, cutlery, and serving spoons is awkward. Instead, put the utensils at the end of the buffet, where they're easy to grab with a free hand once all the serving and ladling is done.

Quick Tip

EAT OUTSIDE!

When kids are home for the summer (and grown-ups too, for that matter!), one fun idea is to take advantage of the weather and eat meals outdoors. A picnic in the backyard is a great way to get some sun and to avoid a lot of the meal cleanup you'd otherwise be doing. If you have a backyard grill or firepit, you can even roast hot dogs or make s'mores as a special treat. They're even more fun in the afternoon at home, because it's unexpected!

059
BE READY TO PARTY

It's always a good idea to keep party supplies on hand for impromptu celebrations or those times when you forgot to pick up candles because you were so busy making the cake!

Label a large shoebox "Party Box" and fill it with the necessities.

The box should include candles, balloons, streamers, cake decorating items, and any festive banners you might want to pin up.

Next time you throw a surprise party, you'll have peace of mind knowing that you're well prepared. The only things left to do will be to cook the food and enjoy the fun.

When stocking your party supply box, remember to shop sales and clearance sections after the holidays. Prices for party supplies hit rock bottom during these times.

060
STORE OUTDOOR UTENSILS

Disposable paper products and plastic cutlery are often used for cookouts, birthday parties, or times when you just can't wash another dish. Designate a cabinet or basket in your kitchen to store these items for easy use and cleanup. To avoid being wasteful, consider purchasing reusable melamine dishes in place of the disposable ones, or purchase compostable paper and plastic products so you're not adding to the landfill. These are made from recycled, biodegradable materials, and you can find plates, cups, utensils—you name it. Another option is to buy a cheap set of "real" utensils and keep them with the outdoor supplies. During parties or backyard cookouts, its best to stay away from glass or china. Things can be dropped when you're having fun,

and who wants to clean up shattered glass when you have a patio full of family and friends?

Here's a checklist of what to include with your outdoor entertaining supplies.

OUTDOOR ITEMS

☐ Paper plates
☐ Bowls
☐ Cutlery
☐ Napkins
☐ Plastic cups
☐ Tablecloths
☐ Straws
☐ Cupcake cups (for snacks)
☐ Toothpicks (for finger foods)

WEEK 3
THE DINING ROOM
Challenge

The dining room (or wherever your dining table is located) is where the family usually ends the day, sharing stories and making memories. If you don't use your dining room to eat dinner, it may be the catch-all space for your family. Or you might only use it for formal occasions. My family eats dinner in there, so we use our dining room every day. Personally, I'd rather get some good use out of it, rather than saving it for fancy dinners or holidays, but I know lots of people who prefer to eat at the kitchen table and use the dining room for bigger groups. Either way, you need it to be organized and functional.

Organizing the dining room is a pretty basic process. If you have a hutch or buffet, you can easily create a functional space for storing necessary items. But if you don't have a hutch, you get to be creative! I could not find a buffet that I liked, so I purchased a long bedroom dresser instead. You might want to reuse a piece of furniture you already own, giving it a fresh coat of paint and a new life in your efficient, organized dining room. Line the drawers and insert bins and organizers to hold necessities for mealtime or entertaining.

THE PROCESS

1. PREPARE
Gather four bins for sorting items into categories. You'll want one for each of the following: Keep, Donate, Trash/Recycle, and Other Room.

2. SORT
Go through everything on the table and buffet, and in all the drawers, and shelves. Place each item into the appropriate bin, purging as much clutter as you can. If you have sixteen candlesticks and haven't lit a taper candle in years, you can probably give those up. Then, place the bins in another room until you are ready to reorganize.

3. CLEAN
The room should now be empty of everything but the furniture. It's time to give it a good cleaning! Scrub the floors, table, chairs, baseboards, buffet, mirrors, windows, and so forth.

4. ORGANIZE
Now it's time to bring the "Keep" bin back and sort it out. Go through the bin one item at a time, sorting by category and putting the items away in drawers or baskets, on shelves, or in display cases. Below are some categories you could use to sort the things going into your hutch.

- ☐ Disposable dishes and cutlery
- ☐ Napkins and napkin rings
- ☐ Placemats
- ☐ Tablecloths
- ☐ Beverage service
- ☐ Seasonal linens

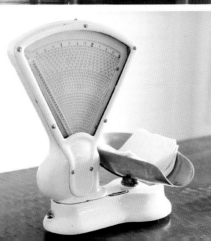

Living + Storage

Well-organized living and work spaces truly make our lives easier. Clearly labeled containers and a thought-out cleaning schedule will add up to less time looking for things and less clutter to tackle. Of course, perfectly labeled toy bins are not a guarantee that your home will remain clean and neat—but they will ease the pain of nighttime pick-ups. Your kids will at long last know where to put things away (without direction or, worse, nagging). In this section, we will cover the foyer, living room, master bedroom, guest room, kids' rooms, closets, and bathrooms. Whether you live in a small city apartment or a sprawling suburban home, you'll be able to implement these organizing tips so you can maximize storage and tackle the chaos of these common spaces once and for all.

061

SET THE TONE FOR YOUR HOME

The foyer is the first space you see each time you enter your home. It should greet you—and others—with open arms. Because this space sets the tone for your home, it needs to be clean, welcoming, and clutter-free at all times. It should also reflect your taste and the general aesthetic of your household. Here are a few tips for sprucing up this space and giving it a warm and inviting feel. After all, you never know when your next guest will drop in.

ESTABLISH A CLEAN SLATE The first and most important step is to deep-clean the space. Empty it completely and scrub it down from top (including the crown molding and light fixtures) to bottom (the floors—including grout, if you have a tiled entryway). Make the whole place shine! Wipe down the front door (inside and outside), all moldings, baseboards, chair rails, doorknobs, locks, mirrors, and walls. Clean up the staircase, dust the rails and surfaces, and wash any rugs or curtains. Next, declutter the hall closet. A clean foyer is the number-one priority when setting the tone for your home, and will make organizing and decorating a fun and enjoyable experience.

CHOOSE THE RIGHT FURNITURE Find a piece of furniture where you can store all of those entryway necessities. Use a piece that will work in your space—maybe a tall chair with a coat rack or a new or repurposed foyer table, if you have room. If you don't have the space, use this same system but set it up in the nearest hall closet or other hallway space. The ideal foyer table has a relatively slim profile, with at least one shelf below for storage. You can also repurpose a dresser for this space, or group some small end tables together.

UPDATE THE RUG You can achieve a massive transformation in your foyer space by updating the rug or runner. Make sure your rug is clean and stylish, free from stains or fraying. As the foyer is the main thoroughfare in your home, this rug will get a lot of use and will show shabbiness sooner than other parts of the space. It works hard, and should be replaced, deep-cleaned, or swapped out every year.

DECORATE After you have your organizing systems in place, it's time to decorate your space. The goal is to exude a welcoming atmosphere. Flowers, candles, a wreath, and a stylish rug make a world of difference.

062

DESIGNATE A PLACE FOR COMMON ITEMS

Keeping a space tidy is just as simple as sorting items into categories. Take the time to really think about which items you use on a daily basis, and then give them a distinct and consistent home that the whole family knows about—and remembers to use.

Where will you store your keys and outgoing mail? Don't spend a lot of time looking for them when you're ready to leave. Use a key holder or hooks to hang them near the door, and place outgoing mail in a wall organizer or in a basket on the foyer table. As for incoming mail, put it in its proper place immediately, so it doesn't pile up. Send any bills straight to the office (see item 118), put catalogs and magazines in their designated spot, and recycle any junk mail before it collects in a useless heap.

063
MAKE OVER THE FOYER

Have you ever walked into someone's house and seen a pile of shoes, bags, coats, and other clutter? It can be distracting and even unwelcoming to visitors. Once you've cleaned and reset your entryway, use these tips to organize the space and make the most of the area. You want it to work in your favor and help streamline the functionality of your home. If you don't have a designated foyer, think about sprucing up the area of your home that people first see when they walk in (see item 064, right).

SORT STORAGE Find a few boxes or baskets for all your foyer items, like handbags, shoes, wallets, scarves, hats, umbrellas, sports gear, school bags, books, keys, and mail (see item 062). Don't let the tabletop become a catchall space for items people drop on their way in the door—the table will become buried almost instantly, you'll never be able to find the item you need, and your organized entryway will go out the window. Label each container and sort the items into categories:

- ☐ Winter wear: Hats, gloves, earmuffs, and scarves.
- ☐ Rain gear: Umbrellas, ponchos, rain boots, etc.
- ☐ Aromatherapy: Candles, wax melts, and lighters.
- ☐ Shoe covers: If you have a "no shoes" rule, keep shoe covers available for guests who cannot take their shoes off.
- ☐ Shopping bags: Keep extra reusable bags or plastic shopping bags on hand.
- ☐ Pets: Cat toys, leashes, doggie bags, and other pet items.

CORRAL COATS & SHOES Keep the hall closet free from clutter. Designate the space for coats, shoes, and bags only—or implement a system that works for your family. We usually keep our coats and shoes in our mudroom. You can also keep a basket and a coat hook near your front door for these items. If you don't have a mudroom, consider creating a space in your garage (see item 065). In my house, shoes equal clutter, so our rule at home is "no shoes in the foyer." My kids carry their shoes to the mudroom or place them in a shoe basket in my husband's office, which happens to be near the foyer. If you don't have a mudroom or are part of a no-shoes household, hang a shoe organizer rack on the inside of the closet door. This will keep shoes off the floor and out of the way. If you don't mind the shoes but want to avoid the dirt, put down a textured mat for feet-wiping, or a pebbled boot tray to drain water—you can DIY one with some river stones for an attractive, no-puddles solution for rainy days.

064
CREATE A FAUX FOYER

Some living spaces just don't lend themselves to a traditional foyer, particularly small homes or railroad-style apartments with long hallways and small rooms. In these homes, your best bet might be to break up your foyer into multiple pieces around your house, with each function handled in its own individual station. Think about how you move through the space when you enter your home, and set up the stations accordingly.

Mount a key rack and mail station on the wall right inside your door. When you come in, the first thing you'll do is hang up your keys and set the mail where it belongs.

Next, you're going to want to take off muddy boots and put your bag down. In a skinny hallway, just shift down a bit from the mail caddy and set up a shoe rack—perhaps one with a shelf for purses and backpacks. Or mount some hooks on the wall above to hang up bags.

Finally, you want to hang up your coat and other outerwear. If there's no coat closet handy, a set of coat hooks and a shelf with a basket for gloves, hats, and scarves is a workable final station.

That's it! Now you're ready to relax in your organized home, without worrying that you'll have lost your gloves, keys, or purse when it's time to rush out to catch the bus in the morning.

065

CREATE A MUDROOM

If you have limited space or no mudroom in your home, consider setting up a mudroom area in the garage. Maximizing how you use this space is key, especially if you have school-age kids (since they come with lots of shoes, coats, book bags, and such). I built this handy organizer to help make a corner of the garage into a functional mudroom. It took me less than an hour to put together, and works like a charm. I really like the 3M Command hooks, but you can use whatever you prefer—just shop around at your local store.

YOU'LL NEED

- ☐ 2 pieces pine board (1 x 4 boards worked for me, but you will need to measure your space to determine what is best for you)
- ☐ Nail gun or hammer and nails
- ☐ 3M Command wood stabilizer strips (or other variety)
- ☐ Decorative trim
- ☐ Paint and paintbrush
- ☐ Scotch extreme fasteners
- ☐ 3M Command hooks (I used the outdoor metal variety)
- ☐ Name tags

STEP ONE Measure the space and determine what lengths of wood you'll need, how many hooks, and so forth. Gather all of your supplies and tools together and be sure everything is within easy reach.

STEP TWO Fasten the pieces of wood together using your nail gun or hammer, then tack on the stabilizer strips. Add decorative trim to the top of your panel.

STEP THREE Paint the wood panel and let it dry. I chose white, to better blend in with the walls and doorway, and because it provides a nice, clean background.

STEP FOUR Hang your panel on the wall with the fasteners, or nail it to wall studs. Then apply the Command hooks to the panel, or screw in hooks of your choosing.

STEP FIVE Label the hooks with each family member's name, and hang up those jackets and accessories! Remember that the hooks will need an hour to cure before you can hang anything up.

066

CHECK OFF THE ESSENTIALS

Whether your mudroom space is a dedicated room in the house or a handy corner of the laundry room or garage, there are a few must-haves that you should be sure to include.

VERTICAL STORAGE Wall-mounted baskets are great for shopping bags, umbrellas, and other frequently used items. You can also use one as a spot for outgoing mail. A shelf with high-up bins can hold seasonal outerwear for when it's needed.

BASKETS A nice basket can hold spare kids' shoes and rain items.

BOOT TRAY In regions that get snow or rain, a boot tray is essential to keep those wet wellies from making a mess.

RUGS A rag rug or doormat keeps kids (and grown-ups!) from tracking dirt and leaves into the house.

And don't forget to add some homey décor touches. I painted the steps and added mailbox numbers, because I love the look. A wall clock really helps to anchor the area, and a few pieces of art or a cluster of family photos can give the space a nice, finished look. A wreath is another great addition!

067

USE THE STAIRS

A staircase and its landings often go unused in terms of storage, but if you have a small entryway, they add huge storage potential for those essential grab-and-go items. In my old home, I used a cubby-and-bin system to store essentials on the stair landing. Decorative bins that match the décor can make a great focal point when you walk into the house. Slim baskets on the stairs are also a great way to keep things handy without adding clutter. You can even assign a bin or basket to each family member, for items that collect downstairs but need to go upstairs at the end of each day.

WEEK 4
THE LAUNCH PAD
Challenge

THE LAUNCH PAD IS THE PLACE
where you set your things down
when you walk in the door, hang the
family calendar, track the chore
chart, store backpacks, drop the car
keys, and so on. It's the hub of an
organized home and can be a
massive clutter magnet. If you don't
have a launch pad, now's a great time
to create one for your family. You
can set it up in your foyer or
mudroom—but it could work in a
kitchen, garage, or hallway, too. It
doesn't have to be a big space, it just
needs to be well organized.

THE PROCESS

1. PREPARE
Gather six bins, one for each of the following:
- ☐ Keep
- ☐ Donate/Sell
- ☐ Trash/Recycle
- ☐ Other Room
- ☐ Shoes
- ☐ Accessories

2. SORT
Sort through everything in the space—absolutely *everything*. It should be empty, except for furniture and the bins, by the time you're done. Each item goes into one of the six bins (if your needs are different, add more bins or change the categories to suit). Purge the items you no longer want, use, love, or need. Get rid of as much clutter as you can.

3. CLEAN
Do a thorough cleaning: Vacuum or mop the floor and wash any rugs. Wipe down the door, baseboards, doorknobs, and switch plates. Wipe down all shelving. Dust any and all lamps and light fixtures. Get into every nook and cranny!

4. ORGANIZE
Now it's time to go through everything in the bins. Put the "Other Room" items where they belong. Toss the trash in the trash can and take it out. Place donations in your car and "to sell" items in the garage to await your next yard sale or Craigslist photo shoot.

5. CHECKLIST
Here are some items that can find a new home in your launch pad:
- ☐ Shoes
- ☐ Backpacks, briefcases, and purses
- ☐ Keys
- ☐ Reusable grocery bags
- ☐ Umbrellas
- ☐ Calendars
- ☐ Jackets and coats
- ☐ Cold weather accessories
- ☐ Dog-walking items
- ☐ Mail
- ☐ Chore charts
- ☐ Electronic charging cords

Store remote controls in hollow book boxes on the coffee table, and add an heirloom quilt for a vintage touch.

068
LOVE YOUR LIVING ROOM

For many people, the living room is the home's central communal space. It's the primary shared area, and the one place where the whole family gets together on a regular, casual basis, whether to lounge or simply watch the evening news.

Some may carve out a corner to create a home office or crafting space, or make the room multitask as a playspace for their children, a gaming and recreation room, a media center with a big-screen TV or movie projector, or even a "man cave" for a bachelor lifestyle.

And for those few who have the square footage and more formal sensibilities, the living room proper is off-limits except for formal entertaining occasions.

However your family uses this adaptable space, organization is key for keeping it clutter-free and useful. Once you set up the living room into specific zones and systems (see item 070), you'll eliminate clutter and give your family a wonderful gift—a peaceful atmosphere in which to enjoy each other's company.

069
DEVELOP A CLEAN ROUTINE

Your cleaning routine will vary depending on how many people (and pets) live with you, your usage patterns, and any allergy concerns, but a general industry standard for carpet is to vacuum high-traffic areas once per week per person living in the household. That means a family of four is supposed to vacuum four times a week! Since that's not realistic for everyone, just make sure to hit the spots that collect dirt with some regularity. Vacuum under your couch cushions every week or two, and wash the slipcovers and pillows seasonally. Dust your blinds (try a rag and white vinegar mixed with water) every week or other week, and wash the curtains twice a year. Don't forget to vacuum under furniture—once a month should do the trick.

070

GET IN THE ZONE

No matter how large or small a room is, looking at it as a series of zones is a great way to reduce clutter and maximize the room's functionality. This is true of every room in the house, but since the living room is used for so many different purposes, the zone system is perhaps most important and effective here. Before you even start thinking about how to divide up the space, give it a thorough cleaning. Get rid of anything you don't like or use, remove items that belong in other rooms, take out the trash, and in any other way you can, simplify the space. Now you're ready to define your zones.

A. READING AREA If your family loves to read, set up a reading corner in the room. Place a comfortable chair and lamp in the space, with a bookshelf nearby. Display books on the shelf, organized by genre, placing the children's books at the very bottom for easy reach. Place a basket by the chair to collect newspapers and magazines for recycling.

B. MEDIA CENTER This space includes movies and DVD players, music CDs, and video gaming equipment. Place game equipment into labeled baskets, and place a tray on the coffee table to store the remote controls. It gives the space a more tidy look—and you'll always know where to find all the various electronics.

C. MEMORIES & KEEPSAKES Store photo albums and keepsakes neatly together on bookshelves. Consider replacing old or mismatched photo albums.

D. TOYS AND HOBBIES Board games, toys, playing cards, knitting projects, and the like can be stored in storage ottomans or on shelving, inside baskets. Storing things out of sight keeps the space looking clutter-free.

E. SITTING AREA Where you place your furniture will depend on how your family uses it. If your family loves watching television and movies, the TV (or screen for the projector) will be the focus of your living room. Move the sofa and chairs to face the TV, but make sure their occupants can still converse. If your family plays a lot of card or board games around the coffee table, you'll want to cluster chairs or floor cushions nearby. And if you're a family of conversationalists, move the couch and chairs to face each other. To streamline the space, store extra blankets or pillows out of sight.

Built-ins are an organizer's best friend, but knick-knacks can add up and clutter the space. Keep your shelving streamlined and simple.

071
REORGANIZE YOUR BOOKSHELF

Gather all of the books in your home and place them in one central location. Sort through each book, categorizing as suits your storage scheme (perhaps by color, genre, or size) and purging those you no longer need. Once you've sorted through, replace them on your bookshelf. Consider only keeping the books that you will read or refer back to later. In the future, when you plan to purchase a new book, use the "one in, one out" rule. If you purchase one, donate one. This eliminates clutter and alleviates storage issues.

072
CATALOG DVDS

Collect all DVDs in the house. Make sure you gather them from kids' rooms as well as the entertainment center or media room. Sort through, donating whatever no longer interests your family. As with your books, categorize the movies in whatever way you please—I suggest sorting by genre (family/kids, drama, comedy, romantic, holiday, horror)—and then create a catalog system as follows.

STEP ONE Using paper or plastic DVD sleeves, transfer the movies from their original plastic case, then number each sleeve.

STEP TWO Index your movies on a catalog sheet in alphabetical order, including the number on the sleeve. (If you're a film buff, you can also include the year of release or the director.)

STEP THREE Toss the cases and store the covers in a small basket or box. This saves valuable space, and by the time you are ready to donate the movies, they won't be of much value—so there's really no need to keep the cases.

073

CONQUER THE CLUTTER

The living room is one of the hardest spaces to keep from getting cluttered, since it's where everyone goes to relax—often with a book or a movie or a crafting project. It's as if the room is begging you to clutter it up. But you can fight back!

PUT IT BACK My house has a "no toys left in the living room" rule, and my kids know to bring their things back to the playroom before bedtime. Similarly, if you're knitting while watching TV, don't just put the project down and walk away. Store your supplies somewhere tidy but close at hand, like in a basket on a nearby shelf.

GROUP LIKE WITH LIKE Stash essential items so that you can lay your hands on them easily—without having to lay your eyes on them all the time. Group similar items into categories (remotes, magazines, blankets, neck or back pillows), and store them together in a basket, bin, tray, or caddy.

CLIMB THE WALLS If your living room lacks shelves, consider hanging baskets on the walls to hold magazines, charging cords, or other such objects. If your living room is also your launch pad (see item 064), mount a basket for mittens, hats, and scarves right by the door, so they're there when you need them—rather than scattered around the house.

TAKE A MOMENT Whenever you walk into or out of your living room, take a moment to notice if anything's out of place and, if it's easy to fix, just do it right then and there, while you're thinking about it. That means folding the blanket and stashing it in a bin, reshelving books, taking your teacup back to the kitchen, and otherwise keeping chaos at bay, one step at a time.

074

MAKE FURNITURE DO DOUBLE DUTY

It seems like furniture designers have finally realized that people have a lot of stuff—and they need somewhere to put it! If storage is limited in your house, or if you find yourself with a lot of items that you use frequently enough that it would be silly to stash them in the basement or attic, you might be able to hide them in plain sight. Here are some clever options.

BENCH WARMER Padded benches are often suggested as a versatile furnishing choice for smaller rooms, as they take up less space than a couch or loveseat. Many benches also do double duty as storage spots, either under a lift-up seat like a traditional piano bench, or behind a chic skirt. Some modern versions simply put the bench on top of shelves or cubicles, so you can display books or keepsakes low to the ground.

SOFA SECRETS Cleverly constructed couches offer under-arm consoles for all of those things you don't want to get up and go fetch once you're comfy, while others sit on top of slide-out drawers or under-cushion compartments.

SHELF HELP Sometimes it doesn't take much to make a big difference in a piece of furniture's utility. A coffee table with cubbies underneath it, or an end table with a shelf or two near the ground, can help contain items that get scattered or look messy.

OTTOMAN EMPIRE The humble footstool can be a multitasking superhero. There are many models that include storage space in addition to their footrest capabilities—from cubes that open up to stash lots of goodies to more elegant pieces with hidden compartments. And when you suddenly have more guests than chairs, an ottoman makes a great casual seat.

075
BUILD IN STORAGE

If you're lucky, your home came with built-in storage in every corner—but if not, you can add built-in fixtures through means as simple as a bookshelf and some crown molding. If you're not handy, hire an expert— the right person won't just build some shelves, they'll help you customize a unique storage solution.

For example, if you have a ton of books and no library to store them in, built-in bookshelves can transform a room. So as not to overwhelm the space, consider floor-to-ceiling shelves with a relatively shallow depth. The minimal footprint preserves floor space and opens up vertical storage for books, media, keepsakes, and baskets of items that would otherwise be taking up valuable tabletops, counters, and desks. The same can be true of display spaces for collectibles or curiosities.

Another popular built-in solution is to add a window seat to an otherwise underutilized wall. This gives you a nice place to sit and read a book, with the bonus of providing shelves or cubbies for stashing that book and all its friends.

For a storybook feel, combine the two ideas and frame a window with bookshelves on either side, with a seat in between. This is a great look for a kid's room or library, tucked into a stairwell, or in any free space where storage is at a premium.

076

LIVE LARGE IN A SMALL SPACE

The living room is the space where we spend most of our time, and, especially in a small house or apartment, it's almost always a multi-use space. If one singular space functions as your playroom, home office, family room, and chill-out space, controlling clutter and using every bit of floor or wall to its best advantage are absolutely crucial. Here are some ideas to get you started.

LOVE YOUR LAYOUT Think about traffic flow in the room and how it's most used. Can you put your office space in an alcove or corner where you can tune out the rest of the room and really focus? If you entertain frequently, be sure that sofas and chairs are grouped well for conversation. If your living room is long and narrow, visually divide it into two conversation zones by using a rug in one space and grouping furnishings accordingly.

MULTITASK FURNISHINGS Get creative with how you use furniture. Storage ottomans help you stash things out of sight, and also serve as additional seating for casual gatherings (see item 074). Use a funky chest instead of a table in order to store extra textiles, or look into coffee tables that lift up to become a dining or work table if needed. If you have overnight guests often, consider a stylish futon (they do exist) or pull-out sofabed.

MINIMIZE ELECTRONICS A wall-mounted flat-screen TV saves space, and a good laptop can easily replace a bigger desktop computer. Use your phone or tablet to stream music to Bluetooth speakers, and you won't have to find space for a bulky stereo.

077

FURNISH A COZY ROOM

In a tiny living room, every piece of furniture needs to be carefully considered. In general, you want to keep things light and eliminate bulk wherever possible.

SHOW SOME LEG The more floor space is visible, the bigger a space seems. Choose chairs, tables, and sofas with legs that elevate them above the ground, and avoid old-fashioned skirted designs. Nesting tables with slender legs are a versatile way to save space and expand surfaces when needed. Choose tall floor lamps to avoid using precious table space, or go for wall sconces for the ultimate in space-saving economy.

MIX IT UP You might be tempted to keep everything small, but one big accent piece can really give a room character. It could be a big piece of art or an oversized chair. Look for furniture with an eye to versatility. An armoire might make a cool desk, with kids' toys stored in the drawers.

GET CLEAR Glass-topped tables vanish into the room and help things feel less crowded. For a retro look, check out clear acrylic end tables. A couple of cubes can make a small coffee table, double as storage, and be easily stashed away.

GO VERTICAL If you can, look at adding tall, slender bookshelves to your space. This profile makes the ceiling feel higher. If you have the time and budget, try making them look built-in (see item 075).

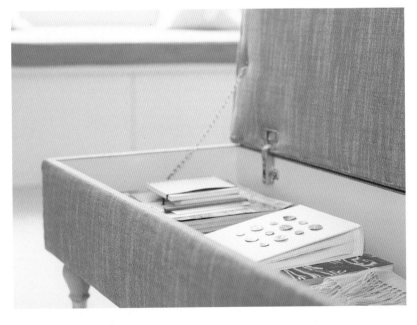

From Toni

Anna Moseley shares helpful homekeeping, decorating, and cleaning tips over at her website askannamoseley.com.

ASK ANNA

" When we moved into our house, these built-in bookshelves were so big—and so ugly—that I was overwhelmed and not sure what to do with them. After trying to ignore them for over a year, I decided that enough was enough. They needed to get organized.

To inspire myself, I gave them a fresh coat of paint. Once they weren't so ugly, it was easy to organize them. I grouped similar books together and arranged them on the shelves. I also grouped "loose" items, like fabric, pictures, and office supplies, in inexpensive baskets. After all my stuff was organized on the shelves, I shopped my house to find decorative items to make the built-ins look even nicer. I am so pleased with how they turned out, and it has been so easy to keep them organized—and pretty—because everything has its place on the shelves. "

BEFORE

WEEK 5
THE LIVING ROOM
Challenge

The living room is probably the most used room in the house, so it can get cluttered fast! One of the ways I've been able to keep our living room clean and organized is by purging as much as possible and only keeping the necessities in the room. I don't allow toys in my living room, because we're lucky enough to have a playroom. But even if you don't have the space to put toys in other areas of the house, you can use footstools, baskets, large bins, and the like to keep them hidden when not in use. Here's how to take your living room from cluttered catchall to streamlined seating area in no time at all.

THE PROCESS

1. PREPARE
Before you begin, do a quick 5–10 minute cleanup of the space. Toss the trash and put things where they belong. Next, gather four bins or boxes, one for each of the following: Keep, Donate, Trash/Recycle, Other Room.

2. SORT
Sort through everything in the room—every single item on the shelves or the floor, in drawers, on tables, and so on. Divide it all into the bins (add more categories if needed). If you have the space, place the bins in a nearby room so you have an empty space to clean and organize. Get rid of as much clutter as you can.

3. CLEAN
Do a thorough deep-clean of the room. Clean the windows, blinds, frames, and any mirrors. Wipe down doors, baseboards, doorknobs, and switch plates. Wipe down and dust all furniture. Remove couch cushions and vacuum underneath. Fluff throw pillows and wash as needed. Pull the couch away from the wall and vacuum under and behind it. Vacuum and/or mop floors. Clean the ceiling fan and lamps or lighting fixtures. Take a lint roller to your lampshades to pick up lurking dust bunnies.

4. ORGANIZE
Deal with the "Trash," "Donate," and "Other Room" boxes. Now, it's time to go through everything in the "Keep" box. Remove one item at a time, categorizing it as you go. You can use a different shelf, basket, or drawer for each category. Keep similar items together. When you're done categorizing, put everything away where it belongs. Here are some categories to consider:

- ☐ DVDs and CDs
- ☐ Candles, lighters, incense, essential oils
- ☐ Throw blankets
- ☐ Remote controls
- ☐ Magazines
- ☐ Toys
- ☐ Books

gather

You

make

me

proud

LA POSTE
FRANC

078
REFRESH YOUR BEDROOM

The master bedroom should be a sanctuary: a place for relaxation, not stress. If yours is bursting with clothes, extra linens, work papers, kids' toys, and other nonessential items, you are likely in dire need of a refresh. Luckily, it won't take more than an afternoon of your time.

Work in one area at a time, clearing out anything that doesn't belong in a bedroom, donating anything you no longer need or use, and storing anything that needs to be properly corralled. Remember that less is more, and be methodical. Reading chairs, ottoman benches, and door hangers can become magnets for clothes and bags that didn't make it to their proper places. Move the stray items to their proper homes, and watch your bedroom become your domain of peace and calm once more.

079
TAKE ADVANTAGE

There will never be a better time to deep-clean your bedroom. Clean the windows, doorknobs, moldings, and baseboards—all those spots that go neglected—and then vacuum and dust. Wash the bed linens, curtains, and bedskirt. Give it a good refresh as you work on the makeover.

080 REST EASY

The master bedroom is a place to relax and recharge for the next day ahead. You want it to be a peaceful and restful location in your home, with as few distractions and stressors as possible. After all, it's where you're supposed to get a good night's sleep. There are a few ways you can rejuvenate and find harmony within this space.

WASH LINENS WEEKLY It takes time and effort, but if you make it a habit to wash your bedding every week, you will slip into those sheets each night with a feeling of calmness and relaxation.

PUT IT ALL AWAY Clutter creates anxiety, which is the opposite of peacefulness. By simply cleaning up after yourself, you will remove the negativity associated with the mess.

DIFFUSE SOME LAVENDER Lavender is a natural alternative to sleep agents. Diffuse the essential oil or spray it on your pillows right before bedtime for a good night's rest (see item 081).

SHUT DOWN THE SCREENS Turn off the television, put away the tablet, and don't look at social media or e-mail on your phone right before bed. Read a book or play calming music, instead. This allows you to unwind, settling your brain rather than pelting it with electronic stimuli right before it's supposed to shut down and get a good snooze.

081 MAKE A DIY LINEN SPRAY

Use this linen spray to usher all your senses into a restful state.

YOU'LL NEED

- ☐ 1 tablespoon isopropyl alcohol
- ☐ 20 drops lavender essential oil
- ☐ Filled bottle of distilled water

In a 4-oz (0.1-liter) glass bottle, combine all ingredients. Blend together by shaking the bottle, and shake well before each use. Spray on pillows and sheets before you get into bed for a restful night's sleep.

082 FIND STORAGE EVERYWHERE

If you live in a small home or you're lacking essential storage or closet space in your bedroom, you can implement under-bed storage. Many beds come with built-in drawers, but you can modify your existing bed, too. Add casters to the bottom of wooden boxes to create rolling drawers that fit neatly beneath the bedskirt, or purchase flat plastic bins for storing shoes, out-of-season clothes, sheets, and blankets.

Storage ottomans can be used in the bedroom, too—use one at the foot of the bed to store extra bedding, and it will become a functional part of your bedroom. Some are even specially designed for shoe storage, with dividers or pockets to hold pairs of dress shoes or sneakers.

083
DIVIDE YOUR DRESSER

The dresser is not only a place to keep clothing—it can also be used to corral jewelry, accessories, wallets, clutches, and more. If you're short on closet space, consider expanding your storage into your dresser drawers so you can maximize bedroom organization.

SORT JEWELRY If you don't have a designated jewelry box (or if yours is overflowing), the top drawer of your dresser is a great alternative. Line it with velvet fabric and insert shallow acrylic organizers to contain earrings, bracelets, and rings. See item 084 for more jewelry organization systems.

DIVIDE DRAWERS One large drawer may not be suitable for smaller articles of clothing. We spend a lot of time folding and putting laundry away, only to find the drawers in complete chaos a day or two later. Using dividers or bins, eliminate drawer chaos by sorting like items into categories (shirts, shorts, tanks, socks, pajamas, and so on). The trick is to fold them all in the same manner and into similar sizes, and then put them away in neat rows, standing up. This is the Konmari method, which will make it much easier to find what you're looking for—plus, clothing will remain organized for longer periods of time.

ROLL UP ACCESSORIES Things like belts, ties, and scarves can be neatly rolled up and placed together in drawer organizers. This is the perfect accessory solution for those of us with small closets. It also extends the life of silk ties, which can suffer indentations from tie hangers.

084
STORE BAUBLES

If you don't have a spare drawer to hold your jewelry, there are plenty of trays, racks, and dishes that are meant to sit on the dresser top and show off your gems. Here are a few more options.

HOOKS Hang simple hooks on the wall above your dresser top or on either side of the vanity mirror, and loop a necklace or bracelet on each.

WALL-MOUNTED DISPLAYS Craft a portable option with corkboard tiles and pins in a frame; or use a small section of chicken wire or perforated metal to hold earrings.

RING DISHES Pick up a small, curved dish—many have a center spike specifically designed to hold rings—and keep one on your nightstand and one in the kitchen, so you'll always know where to look.

OVER-THE-DOOR RACK Many retailers sell over-the-door jewelry racks for those with heftier collections. Hang one on the inside of a closet door, and pick out your jewelry alongside your outfit.

BEHIND THE MIRROR A recent innovation in hidden storage, some standing and wall-mounted mirrors are built on hinges—simply swing the mirror open, and you have a vertical jewelry storage case.

TIERED PLATES Repurpose a kitchen item for the dresser top: a tiered serving platter can make for excellent bracelet storage, making the most of little-used vertical space.

085
KEEP AN OPEN MIND

In a small space, don't assume that everything has to be hidden in order to maintain an organized room. As long as everything has a designated spot, you can put things away even when they remain out in the open. For example, open shelving (popular in kitchens and dining rooms) can work in a bedroom, too, where you might have stylish wardrobe items that deserve to become part of the décor. Hook your fabulous high heels over picture rails or strips of molding mounted on the wall. Keep your perfume bottles on a decorative tray, or store silk scarves in a colorful, neat stack. If there's no room in the closet, buy a pretty hamper with a cover, or hang one to save floor space. Figure out what works best for your space.

THE MASTER BEDROOM
Challenge

Do you have endless "stuff" shoved under the bed, messy drawers, and clothes laying wherever there is an open space? If you said yes, you most definitely need this challenge.

Your master bedroom is your haven; once this space is clean and organized, you'll have the oasis you deserve to retire to at the end of the day. My motto for the master bedroom is "less is more." You don't need very much stuff in a bedroom. Keep this in mind when cleaning and organizing. Note that we are not cleaning out the closet this week, only the bedroom. The closet gets its turn next week.

THE PROCESS

1. PREPARE
Find five laundry baskets, or good-sized boxes, and label them with your sorting categories: Keep, Trash, Donate, Clothes (all the clothes that will be staying in the bedroom), and Other Room.

2. EMPTY IT OUT
Concentrating on one hot spot at a time, empty the space completely. Here are your main zones to focus on, though you'll be evaluating everything in the room.

Under the Bed Pull everything out from under the bed and sort it into the baskets. This space should be empty.

Dresser Drawers Empty all of the drawers onto the bed. Go through each piece of clothing carefully, and consider its usefulness. Does it fit? Do you still wear it? If not, donate it! Fold and place the remaining clothes back into the drawers, with like items together.

Nightstands Empty out the drawers and take everything off the top. Clean the surface off, wipe it down, and only put back the necessities.

Dresser Top This is a clutter hot spot, and it's the first area people notice when walking into the bedroom, so you really want to keep it clean. Sort every item out into your baskets. Wipe the surface down and put back only necessary items.

3. CLEAN
Vacuum and dust thoroughly, and clean the windows, doorknobs, and baseboards. Also wash the bed linens, curtains, and bedskirt.

4. ORGANIZE
This is the fun part—as well as the key to keeping the room clean. Use baskets and bins to place like items together around the room. If everything has a home, it's more likely to find its way back to it on a regular basis—saving you the hassle of constantly tidying.

5. ENJOY
That's it. You're finished! Now light a candle and enjoy your sanctuary.

086

PREPARE THE GUEST BEDROOM

Show your guests how much you care by making their stay as cozy and inviting as possible. Maintaining an organized system for guests will take some of the stress out of preparing for visitors. Nothing says welcome to your home like a hotel-inspired guest bedroom or, better yet, a suite with a private bathroom or sitting area. If you have a designated guest bedroom, there's so much you can do to transform this space into a luxury accommodation for your guests. Consider including the following components.

LUXURIOUS LINENS High-end bedding like an Egyptian cotton sheet set, especially in white, gives the room a more formal, hotel-like feel. Get the highest thread count you can afford and make sure to include at least four pillows.

COMFORT ITEMS Add a throw blanket, extra robe, and slippers to the bedside. If you have space, add a reading chair, desk, and lamp.

SNACK STATION On the dresser, you can set up a self-serve snack station. Include bottles of water, champagne and glasses, a mini coffee maker, coffee and tea, elegant coffee cups (monogrammed would be a great touch), and a small basket of snacks (chocolate, crackers, granola bars) for late-night hunger pangs.

READING MATERIAL A current newspaper and a few magazines add to the hotel experience.

MISCELLANEOUS ITEMS Make sure your guests have helpful items like an alarm clock, TV channel guide, and the guest WiFi password.

087

STOCK YOUR BATHROOM FOR GUESTS

Create a spa-like atmosphere in your guest bathroom with a few simple touches. If you don't have a separate guest bathroom, you can designate a guest cabinet or shelf in a personal bathroom. My guest bathroom is a part of my teenager's bathroom—it works surprisingly well for us. There are a number of things you can do to create an inviting experience for your guests—and while you may feel some of these go beyond what's necessary, simply pick and choose your favorites and leave the rest.

INVITING DÉCOR Clutter-free, neutral décor in the bathroom always satisfies.

CLEAN TOWELS Consider keeping a separate set of white bath towels, hand towels, and washcloths specifically for guests. It's always nice to get a matching set.

TOILETRIES Stock up on extra toiletries. You never know what your guests may have forgotten, so include everything! You can find inexpensive travel-size toiletries at big chain stores or dollar stores. Or, when you stay at a hotel, bring home the extra toiletries and add them to your supply:

- ☐ Toilet paper
- ☐ Disposable razors
- ☐ Shaving cream
- ☐ Toothpaste
- ☐ Toothbrushes
- ☐ Floss
- ☐ Shampoo and conditioner
- ☐ Deodorant
- ☐ Soap
- ☐ Lotion
- ☐ Hairspray
- ☐ Eye makeup remover
- ☐ Mouthwash
- ☐ Feminine products
- ☐ First-aid kit
- ☐ Comb and brush
- ☐ Cotton balls and swabs

HAMPER Designate a separate hamper just for guest clothes. Once it's full, offer to do a load, or point them to the laundry room if they prefer. Remember, you want to pamper your guests and make them feel like they're on vacation!

Use white linens and add fresh flowers to make a guest room feel extra luxurious and welcoming.

088

MAKE YOUR GUESTS FEEL WELCOME

When guests come to visit, we want them to feel as welcome as possible. In my house, this includes pampering them with a well-stocked kitchen and an array of entertainment options to choose from.

MENU PLANNING Before your guests arrive, find out if they have any food or environmental allergies. Also ask what their favorite snacks, foods, and drinks are. Keep a basket of snacks and fruit on the kitchen counter so they can grab and go as they please. Plan out the dinner menu ahead of time and go shopping before your guests arrive. And last but not least, display the weekly menu on the refrigerator door for all to see. You'll head off unforeseen issues this way, or your guests can make alternate plans without feeling awkward. The more organized you are, the more smoothly your week of hosting will go.

ENTERTAINMENT Visit your local tourism welcome center or chamber of commerce and collect all of the fliers about activities that your area has to offer. You never know what your guests may want to do, so it's best to be prepared ahead of time, and they may want to do some research on their own. Be prepared and research ahead of time so you can give them an array of options.

089

CREATE A GUEST HAVEN

If you live in a small home or don't have a designated bedroom for your guests, you can still pamper them by putting together a guest basket. They'll feel just as pampered on the pull-out sofabed if they can tell you've prepared and are eager to have them.

Use a version of the guest bedroom list (see item 086), modified to fit the limitations of your space (and the size of your basket!). Offer freshly laundered blankets and sheets, a set of travel-size toiletries, and an extra toothbrush (just in

case). If you can, give them a place to keep their things, such as a designated closet or dresser, or set up a luggage rack for their suitcase. An extra chair can perform this job just as well, and will help keep their things from being in the way.

090

IMPROVISE A NIGHTSTAND

In a one-bedroom apartment or small space where your guests are sleeping in the living room or den, it can be difficult to provide them with the amenities of a true bedroom. Start with the guest basket (see left) and use a folding tray table, chair, or even a stack of big books to improvise a nightstand. (You can strap them together with a leather belt, or nestle them in a box.) Your guests will need somewhere to put their glasses and charge their phone while they sleep, and they'll appreciate your thoughtfulness!

091

PLAN A PERFECT NURSERY

Organizing a nursery begins a little differently than many other rooms—your first focus is safety, then ease of use, and finally, a decorating scheme.

THINK SAFETY Baby-proofing is of primary importance, and the process will change as your child grows. Consulting a professional is optimal, but you can get a head start by kneeling down to your child's level to find any sharp edges that need to be padded. Anchor all large furniture in place, and install childproof latches and baby gates where needed.

INSTALL UTILITY LIGHTING The nursery is the site of many different vital tasks, so a variety of lighting options will come in handy. Install a dimmer switch so you're less likely to disturb a sleeping child when you check in at night. Make sure there is ample lighting near rocking chairs and changing tables, and always make sure cords are out of reach of the little ones.

MIX UP THE STORAGE Large drawers and baskets can make it easy to misplace tiny items. Look for drawer organizers and bins which take clothing sizes into consideration.

BE PRACTICAL When decorating, choose bedding and window coverings first, and adjust paint colors and accessories to suit.

092

USE AN ANTIQUE ARMOIRE FOR BABY

An armoire may seem like a very adult piece of furniture, but an old antique can be fitted up as a perfect closet for baby clothes.

Ideal for nurseries that don't have a closet—or have one that's so large it's better suited for storage than swallowing up tiny onesies—an armoire can usually fit multiple racks of pint-sized pieces. You could even use simple tension rods, as small baby clothes don't tend to weigh very much.

Remove the doors entirely for neat, open storage (you could even sort all those cute little clothes by color), or leave them on for a surprisingly sophisticated addition to your baby's new abode.

Mix and match storage options to suit your child's needs. A fresh coat of bright paint on an old dresser can make for a brand new piece.

094
MAKE A PLAY CORNER

Your kids' interests and passions should extend to their other spaces around the home, as well. Play spaces and study corners should reflect their interests—they'll take more pride in these areas, and so will you. If you have younger kids who need supervision, and they spend a lot of time with you in common areas of the house (such as the kitchen or home office), it's a good idea to set up a play corner for them in these rooms. Use bins, crates, or lockers to keep a few select toys in this area, and put down a comfy rug or mount some fun wall art to designate the space. Now they can play on their own while you work, cook, or get things done around the house.

093
DESIGN A FUNCTIONAL CHILD'S ROOM

After babyhood, your children will develop opinions of their own. When decorating and organizing kids' rooms, make sure to involve them throughout the entire process—from planning to implementation. They need to know that their voice and decisions matter—and it makes a world of difference when it comes to maintaining a clean room later on.

FIND OUT WHAT THEY LOVE
What are your kids' hobbies? What do they spend their free time tinkering with? Take some time to observe their habits. Find out what makes them tick. Once you know what they truly value, set up their space around that theme. Once you do, they will take pride in having a clean space.

ORGANIZE LIKE A CHILD Get down to your kids' eye level and find out what they see. Can they reach

their toys and books? Is everything labeled in an age-appropriate way? (For readers, labels are fine, but for little kids, use pictures or symbols.) Make sure you are organizing the space with them in mind.

SIMPLIFY THE SPACE Clear out anything that is not being used. Arrange furniture to allow for maximum floor space. Get rid of all visual clutter in the room.

SET THEM UP FOR SUCCESS Declutter closets, drawers, and toys monthly. Set up a homework station in the bedroom or elsewhere (see item 124). Keep it simple! Remember, less is more. Hang a calendar (let your child pick it out) over the desk and teach your kids to write in project and homework due dates, after-school activities, and lesson times. Make sure they check their calendars every morning and evening.

095

MASTER YOUR CLOSETS

The master closet can contain all manner of things: clothes, shoes, bags, and everything else. To keep it organized, take control of the clutter and customize your closet to your specific needs. Make sure to purge beforehand in order to gain valuable space and avoid the headache of organizing things you don't use.

CLEAR Set aside some time to clear out your bedroom closet and sort through everything in it.

SORT Divide into four categories: Keep, Repair, Toss, and Donate.

DESIGNATE Identify a spot for everything. If an item doesn't have a home, make one or purge it.

EXPAND Maximize hanging space with double rods—see how the pros at Neat Method did it, at right.

REVERSE Some people prefer to hang pants on the top rack and tops on the bottom one. Figure out what suits your needs.

MATCH Purchase matching hangers for a streamlined look.

NEST Place purses and bags inside each other like nesting dolls.

STORE Put out-of-season clothing into a longer-term storage spot.

EDIT Sort through duplicates and purge the older items.

REPLACE Follow the "one in, one out" rule. If you purchase something new, donate something old.

096 PUT SHOES ON DISPLAY

Shoe clutter is one of the hardest things to get control of—the average woman owns well over 20 pairs! There are endless storage options: get shoes up off the floor and display them on a shelf, either in shoe boxes or neatly arranged in rows. Clear plastic bins keep the dust off and extend the life of shoes—you probably spent a fortune on them, so care for them well!

097

UTILIZE EVERY SPACE

For those with a limited amount of space, it's important to utilize the overlooked areas in your home that can be reimagined as storage. Add hooks, shoe bags, or racks to the backs of doors, install high shelves for items you use infrequently, and use decorative bins or clear containers to store items neatly and provide easy access to their contents. Think creatively about neglected spaces in your home.

Quick Tip

DONATE IT

Keep a donation hamper in the closet (lined with a trash bag). When you no longer want an item, place it in the hamper. Once the hamper is full, donate the bag.

098

STORE CLOTHES SEASONALLY

When the seasons change, it's time to pull out the bathing suits and sundresses (or the wool scarves and coats), but unless you have spacious closets, you're going to have to pack up your seasonal gear to make room for the new items. Remember, the cleaner and more organized your storage, the more pleasant it will be to pull back out next year.

CLEAN, COOL, DARK, AND DRY Your seasonal storage area must incorporate these four elements in order to protect your clothing. Avoid areas near heating systems and moisture to prevent fading or attracting insects.

CREATIVE STORAGE Unused suitcases, or even the clear zip-up bags that comforters come in, can be repurposed as storage. Fill with like items and store out of sight. If you are out of places to hide your boxes or totes, you can stack a few boxes on top of each other and drape a colorful cloth over them, creating a homemade table.

CEDAR CHEST Tight-fitting cedar chests make it difficult for fabric-chomping insects to attack your clothes. Lining the container with acid-free paper will also help.

TIP-TOP CONTAINERS Inspect all of your storage containers to make sure they are free from cracks or stains that could allow your clothes to become damaged.

GROUPED ITEMS In order to make unpacking a breeze during the next season, place all of your sweaters in one container, all your heavy pants in another, coats in a third, and so on. Continue combing through your winter wardrobe until everything has been put away.

ACCESSIBLE AREAS While you'll want to keep your seasonal wardrobe out of the way, keep in mind that you still want this location to be accessible enough so it's not a burden to unpack next season. Some storage containers can easily slide under your bed or couch.

099

COLOR-CODE CLOTHING

Closet organization doesn't end after you've purged and categorized. Go one step further by color-coding clothing to finish off the space. It's pleasing to the eye and gives the space a more uniform and streamlined look. A color-coded wardrobe also speeds things up when you are picking your outfit for the day. It makes it easier to find what you're looking for, especially when you absolutely must locate that special blue sweater.

Quick Tip

REPEL BUGS

Even without a cedar chest, you can ensure pests stay away and keep your seasonal clothing fresh by adding a sheet of fabric softener, mothballs, or small cedar blocks to your containers.

From Toni

Ginny Grover is the expert organizer behind organizinghomelife.com. She shares fabulous DIY, decorating, and organizing projects for all areas of the home.

GINNY **ORGANIZING HOME LIFE**

66 My hubby and I bought a 50-year-old home and have been working on updating it over the last few years. The master closets were reach-in style with very limited space for organizing our things. We were dealing with a single rod, double high shelves, and lots of wasted floor space. (Yikes.) I had been using miscellaneous baskets until we could afford to install a closet organization system—when we did, we evaluated our closets and recognized our unique needs before designing them.

My hubby wears business suits, dress shirts, and pants, and has very few shoes. I, on the other hand, have as many shoes as my closet can handle and have long dresses as well as shorter tops and slacks. The new design works so well for both of our needs and hardly an inch of space is wasted. The closets still look almost exactly like they did right after, because the system works. It's easy to put things away when there is a designated place for each piece. We love it! 99

BEFORE

AFTER

WEEK 7
THE MASTER CLOSET
Challenge

Once your bedroom is clean and organized, it's time to tackle the master closet. For me, it seems like this area always needs to be organized. It's hard to keep it clean all the time, thanks to the amount of stuff—basically, it's a constant struggle.

In our new home, we are blessed to have a huge, master walk-in closet. It fits a lot of stuff, so I knew that I had to find a good system to organize everything. Otherwise, it would quickly spiral out of control. I chose to hang all of our jeans and other bottoms in the closet, as well as all shirts (except T-shirts; I still keep those in my dresser, though some people really prefer hanging them alongside blouses).

If your living space has several closets rather than one big master, you may choose to do them all this week. Don't tackle kids' closets or the linen closet—those are coming up in future weeks.

THE PROCESS

1. PREPARE
Gather up those four baskets you're coming to know so well and label them as always: Keep, Trash, Donate, and Other Room.

2. SORT AND PURGE
Go through everything in the closet, taking every single item out and sorting it into the bins. Really evaluate each item of clothing, as well as bags and shoes if you keep them in this closet. If you don't wear it, or it doesn't fit, or if you're hanging onto old, ragged, or out-of-style items for sentimental reasons, know that someone else might appreciate it much more than you. Go ahead and put it in the "Donate" bin. You'll declutter your closet and make the future recipient happy!

3. CLEAN
Clear everything out of the closet, down to the bare floor, walls, and built-in fixtures, then vacuum or mop the floors, clean the door and doorknobs, and wipe down the shelves and other storage spaces.

4. ORGANIZE
Now it's time to organize. Hang the clothes in sections: short-sleeve tops, long-sleeve tops, pants, skirts, dresses, and so on. Color-code if you are feeling extra ambitious or if you think it will help you locate your items in the future. Organize the shoes, too! If you have a really tiny closet, look into multi-tier hangers and organize by category (one for dressy tops, one for casual tops, and so on for suitable items).

100
TIDY UP KIDS' CLOSETS

Make it a habit to tidy up kids' closets on a weekly basis. Sunday evenings seem to work best for us. It's the start of a new week, and tidying allows the kids to see what's clean, what's dirty, and what they might want to put together as outfits for the week ahead.

HANGERS Remove all empty hangers and take them to the laundry room. After all laundry is finished and clothing is hung, remove the still-unused hangers from the closet. Empty hangers create unnecessary clutter.

CATEGORIES Reorganize clothing into categories and hang like items together. Rehang clothes that have fallen off the hangers.

LOOSE ITEMS Straighten up shoes and accessories.

CLUTTER Move sports equipment to the garage or mudroom and winter coats, outerwear, or gear to the hall closet.

DONATIONS Assess the need for clothing, shoes, and accessories often. Haul away anything that is no longer being used.

101
KEEP TINY SHOES ORGANIZED

Designate a space in the closet for your child's shoes. Depending on the children's ages (and heights), it can be a shelf, door organizer, or basket on the floor. Make sure there is enough room to fit all of the shoes each child owns. Teach them to put their shoes away each day and to tidy them weekly.

102
CONTAIN ACCESSORIES

Belts, bags, hair accessories, and hats can become a whirlwind of clutter in a child's closet. Corral these accessories in baskets or clear shoe boxes and label each clearly. Another method is to hang wall hooks on the side walls in the closet for belts and bags. There are also special hat hangers that can really help out. Keep everything off of the floor (with the exception of a shoe basket) to minimize clutter and keep the closet looking tidy.

103
PERFORM A SEASONAL SWEEP

Remove all out-of-season clothing from the closet. Assess each item's size, condition, and whether your child still needs it. Label a bin with your child's name, the sizes that are being stored in the box, and the season. Launder everything and store the bin on the top shelf of the closet or in the attic. If anything is needed, you'll know where to find it—and if not, you can move it to the donation pile or hand it down to the next recipient.

SUMMER   PAJAMAS   DANCE   VACATI

Kids' clothing has the advantage of being shorter and smaller. You may be able to fit two hanging bars in even a tiny closet.

TOMS

WEEK 8
THE KIDS' CLOSET
Challenge

This week we tackle kids' closets. If you don't have children, I know you want to take this week off—but try to keep the momentum going by organizing another closet in your home!

After the big master closet project you completed last week, this should seem pretty simple—although if you have several kids of various ages, it might take a while.

Organize each child's room and their corresponding wardrobe, belongings, and other stuff one by one, to avoid mixing everything up.

THE PROCESS

1. PREPARE
Get five baskets or bins for sorting, and label them as follows: Fits Now, Bigger Sizes, Giveaway/Donate, Other Room, and Trash.

2. SORT AND STASH
Empty the entire closet and put everything onto the bed. Next, sort through all of it. Only keep what your child wears now or will wear soon. Place clothes that do not fit yet into a tote or basket, and store it up high so your child will not go through it and mess it up. After you are finished sorting, place the "giveaways" in a trash bag and put in your trunk, place the "Other Room" in the hallway until you are finished with the closet, and keep the final baskets (the clothes that your child will wear) by your side.

3. CLEAN
Clear everything out of the closet, down to the bare floor, walls, and built-in fixtures, then vacuum or mop the floors, clean the door and doorknobs, and wipe down shelves and other storage spaces.

4. ORGANIZE
Use baskets and bins to organize things that do not need to be hung up. Sort and label the bins according to your child's needs. For example, mine are labeled as follows: Dance, Gymnastics, Vacation, Pajamas, and Summer or Winter (I have two tags on this basket and switch them out as the season changes). Use shoe organizers to keep shoes looking neat and in good shape. For clothes that go on hangers, separate them by type of clothing (short-sleeve tops, long-sleeve tops, jackets, etc.) and then sort by color. They look so much nicer that way!

104

KEEP LINEN CLOSETS NEAT

Ideally your linen closet will be organized into easily viewable and reachable sections. Thankfully, getting it in order is a fairly easy task.

ASSESS THE CURRENT SYSTEM Stand back and observe the current organizational system you have in place. Is there order—or is there chaos? Does it work for you? Setting up a system with functional organizing in mind helps keep things tidy without a lot of effort.

EMPTY THE SPACE Clear out the closet and start with a fresh canvas. Empty the shelves, drawers, and floor space. Vacuum and wipe down shelving, walls, and baseboards. Purge things you no longer use.

LABEL TO YOUR ADVANTAGE Using a label maker or tags, create categories. Designate where you are going to place your linens so all family members know where to find things and can put things away with minimal guidance. Labeling also helps keep closets neat and streamlines the space. Below are some categories that can be used in the linen closet.

- ☐ Towels: Hand towels, washcloths, and beach towels
- ☐ Sheet sets: Twin, full, queen, king
- ☐ Winter bedding: Flannel sheets, electric blankets, and heavy blankets
- ☐ Throw blankets
- ☐ Quilts
- ☐ Pillows: Extra pillows and pillowcases
- ☐ Curtains: Shower curtains, drapes, etc.
- ☐ Table linens

FOLD LIKE A PRO There are many folding methods that work. Whichever method you choose, remain consistent. Fold all towels and bedding the same way. By doing this, the closet will become more space-efficient and tidy. If you're stymied by how to neatly fold a fitted sheet, see item 105 below.

COLOR-CODE So there's no second-guessing where things go, color-code linens for different areas of the house. For example, assign white for guest towels and gray or blue for family towels.

SET LIMITS Keep only three sets of sheets per bed and three towels and washcloths per person in the household. Pick your favorites and donate or toss all the others.

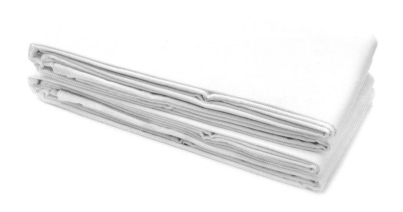

105

FOLD A FITTED SHEET

Folding a fitted sheet is not as hard as it seems. For true perfection, do this on a flat surface, but you can do it standing, too. First, tuck each hand into the pockets of two corners. Bring your hands together and flip one corner over the other so they nest. Do the same with the other corners, so all four are now nested. Now treat the nested corners like a point and fold normally. Voila!

WEEK 9
THE LINEN CLOSET
Challenge

So many closets! By now you should have this closet organization thing down to a fine art. This is the last closet organization in the challenge—next week we'll be heading back to individual rooms. If you don't have a linen closet, you can organize the area where you keep your extra sheets and blankets. Maybe it's a few shelves in the hall closet, or a covered bin in the master. Do what works for you, but keep the system going.

THE PROCESS

1. PREPARE
Get your trusty four bins ready: Keep, Trash, Donate, and Other Room.

2. EMPTY IT OUT
Clear out the space, down to the last dust bunny! Place everything on your bed or on a cleared-off table, away from the closet. If you have to carry everything to the bed jumbled up in laundry baskets, go ahead and do it. You will sort though it soon.

3. CLEAN
Wipe down the shelves, vacuum or mop the floor, and clean the closet door and doorknob. Leave it shiny clean and smelling like lemons (or whatever scent your cleaner of choice leaves behind).

4. SORT & PURGE
Sort through everything that was in the space, and only keep what you really use. Do you really need four sets of sheets for each bed? Do you need 15 pillowcases? Commit to purging unused clutter. You do not need it!
If you are going to use decorative baskets to organize the space, label them according to your personal needs. I have one for each family member's sheets, one for pillowcases, and one for curtains. You may also keep extra towels and such in the linen closet.

5. ORGANIZE
Line up your decorative baskets or designated piles and place like items together. Make sure you have purged extra sheet sets and other things that you do not need. Once you are finished organizing, place your baskets in the linen closet, or line up your sets of linens with like items together on the shelves. Label the shelves if you don't use baskets.

GAVIN'S
Sheets

MASTER
Sheets

Curtains

PILLOW
Cases

ALEX'S
Sheets

GAVIN'S
Sheets

ABIGAIL'S
Sheets

Curtains

A clean bathroom is a welcoming bathroom. The more organized it is, the neater it will stay.

107
THINK ABOUT PROXIMITY

Placement is key when keeping the bathroom clean. Keep your toilet cleaner near the toilet, the daily shower cleaner in the shower, and the sink cleaner below the sink. If it's within reach, you will be more apt to complete the task.

106   CLEAN BATHROOMS DAILY

Being organized doesn't just mean clearing the clutter from drawers and closets. It also means implementing a daily and weekly cleaning routine. Get into the habit of quickly cleaning the bathroom each morning after you've gotten ready for the day. It only takes a few minutes and it's well worth the time and minimal effort it takes. When returning home in the evening, your clean bathroom will be calling your name—perhaps to indulge in a stress-relieving bubble bath. Here's a quick, daily checklist to keep things ready and waiting.

WIPE DOWN Wipe counters and sinks each day. Using a little elbow grease, quickly swipe up any toothpaste messes and countertop mishaps, and remove the toiletry clutter that's bound to accumulate.

SPRAY AND SQUEEGEE Using a daily shower cleaner, spray down shower walls (and doors, if you have them) immediately after showering. This will prevent soap scum buildup. If you have glass doors, pick up a mini squeegee to use after each shower session.

SWISH TOILETS Sprinkle baking soda and a squeeze of Castile soap into the bowl and quickly swish the toilets. This will prevent pesky rings.

PICK UP DIRTY CLOTHES Put laundry in the hamper. Easy enough!

EMPTY THE TRASH IF NEEDED Don't necessarily wait until the trash is full before emptying it, as with other rooms —bathroom trash cans don't fill as quickly as some others, but they can be full of messy or bulky things like sticky containers.

108
KEEP IT FRESH WITH ESSENTIAL OILS

Keep your lavatory smelling fresh by adding a few drops of pure essential oil to a cup of baking soda and placing it behind the toilet. You can also add a few drops to the inside of the cardboard toilet paper roll each time you change it. Finally, add a drop to the trash can when changing the bag. Essential oils work like a charm, and they're much better than chemicals. Lavender is my personal favorite.

109
MAKE THE MOST OF A TINY BATHROOM

In polite society, back when it was considered tacky to use the word "bathroom," people used to refer to "the smallest room in the house." In some houses, and particularly older condos or apartments, that room can be very small, indeed. While a total remodel is often not an option, a few changes can make a giant difference in a tiny space.

OPEN UP THE SPACE Replacing the standard cabinet- or counter-mounted sink with a pedestal or wall-mounted model frees up a ton of floor space, and can be a really clean, contemporary look—but you do lose the storage. In a really small space, consider replacing your toilet and even your bathtub with narrower models.

GET CLEAR Introduce as much glass and as many reflective surfaces as you can. Swapping out an old-fashioned opaque shower stall or shower curtain for a sheet of clear glass can make an amazing difference (and force you to keep that shower sparkly clean!). Maximize your mirrors, too—just don't install one directly across from the commode.

LOSE THE CABINETS Open shelving takes up a lot less space, and lets you show off your color-coordinated towels. Use basket and bins to contain any items you don't really want on permanent display.

PURGE THE CLUTTER Go through every single thing in your bathroom and determine whether or not you really need it. Be ruthless. No matter how expensive that moisturizer was, if you don't use it, it goes out. Look at expiration dates, and ditch anything past its prime.

GET IN THE CORNER Angled spaces are often underutilized, but bathroom accessory designers are getting smart about making them work for you. Shelving units, laundry baskets, and even sinks come pre-fit to squeeze a little more floor space out of your powder room.

110
STORE IT RIGHT

In a tiny bathroom, storage becomes even more important. Think about what absolutely has to be in the room, as opposed to what can live in the linen closet, kitchen, or hall closets. For the things that do belong in the bathroom, get creative with your storage solutions.

KEEP JUST A FEW For things like cotton swabs and cotton balls, store the big packages in a closet and keep just a handful in the bathroom, in small containers.

GO UP Hang a shelf over the bathroom door to squeeze in extra space. Store extra bath towels or beach towels there.

ADD SHELVES Floating shelves can be a good way to add in storage where needed. Consider a hotel-style shelf in the shower to store towels and essentials. If your towels are color-coordinated, they actually add to the décor. Special shelving racks that fit over the commode make use of often-ignored space. And a slim shelf, like a spice rack, might be a perfect solution for toiletries.

LEAN A LADDER A storage ladder adds a fun, contemporary feel and allows you to customize how and where to stash items you need.

USE THE DOORS Use all available doors for storage—hang towels on the back of the bathroom door, and store the hair dryer on the back of the cabinet door.

HOOK IT Use coat hooks instead of a towel bar in a shared bathroom.

111
LIGHTEN UP

Some people intentionally go for dark, bold colors in a small space to make a dramatic statement, but your best bet for maximizing space is a soft, light palette, with just a few pops of color. Use your towels and a few small pieces of art to add zing to an otherwise serene color scheme.

Natural light always makes a space seem bigger, but if you can't bring sunshine in, use accent lighting with natural-spectrum bulbs. A fixture swap can make a big difference: Think about wall-mounted sconces on either side of a vanity. And if you have a single fixture, find something fresh for the spot that reflects your personal decorating style.

112
PAY ATTENTION TO DETAIL

The little touches can transform a relaxing bath into a full-body spa experience. Don't skimp on the details—you're worth it!

SPECIALTY BATH PRODUCTS Exfoliating sponges and gloves, face masks, bubble bath, French-milled soap, and body oils are some of the many products you can use to pamper yourself in this space. A pretty bath caddy keeps essentials at your fingertips.

RELAXING MUSIC Pandora has some fabulous spa stations, including Deuter, Shajan, and Enya. Create a spa playlist and get lost in a calming bubble bath and meditative sonic space at least once a week. Waterproof Bluetooth speakers allow you to safely stream music from your phone.

FINISHING TOUCHES An orchid, a lightly scented lavender candle, and a sophisticated white bathrobe all add a touch of serenity to a home spa bathroom. These tiny elements can really make the difference between an average bathroom and an at-home oasis.

113
TURN YOUR BATHROOM INTO AN OASIS

A bathroom oasis is a divine luxury, and everyone deserves to have one! Here are a few things you can do to create it, whether you have a small or large space—and even if you have to share it with someone who doesn't have your appreciation for pampering.

ELIMINATE CLUTTER To get started on the transformation of your space, the room must be decluttered. Pull everything out of the cabinets, drawers, showers, and closets, and clear the shelves and countertops. Purge expired or empty bottles, and toss the products you never use. Free yourself from product clutter! Have you ever seen a cluttered spa?

FRESHEN UP BATH LINENS Old, worn-out towels and washcloths have to go—they've had their day, and stained and faded bath linens are not spa-worthy. Replace them with fresh, new linens. Remember, you don't have to spend a fortune. There are many discount stores that carry luxurious brands for less than retail prices. You can use old towels and washcloths as cleaning rags, or look into donating them. Vets and animal shelters are often looking for worn but clean towels for bathing animals.

TRANSFORM THE WALLS When choosing a wall color for your spa bathroom, stay away from bold, busy colors. They're great in some spaces, but for the spa-like experience you're going for, opt for a more serene and calming color palette.

114
HEAT THINGS UP

Nothing adds a sense of luxury like a fresh, warm towel—unless, of course, it's stepping out of your bath onto a gently heated floor. You can purchase a warming towel rack for under $50 USD if you shop around, and they need very little electricity to operate. A heated floor is definitely more of a project, but if you're handy (or have a DIY-savvy friend or loved one), an under-tile heating system for your floor can be a weekend project with a wonderfully soothing payoff. Check your local home store for supplies and instructions.

115
WHIP UP A WHIRLPOOL

While installing an in-home Jacuzzi isn't attainable for everyone, there are budget-priced alternatives that can turn any tub into an on-demand whirlpool. Look into immersible jet accessories—as home spas become an everyday luxury for more and more people, the at-home or portable options are increasing. If you're due for a remodel, you can also look into replacing your standard bathtub with a deep soaking tub. The only problem? You might not ever want to get out.

116

KEEP BATHROOM CLOSETS NEAT

The bathroom closet might, in fact, be your linen closet, but in my home, its sole purpose is to store personal care products. These items can really pile up and waste much-needed space. To clear out the excess, begin by emptying the closet completely. Then focus on what you actually use and would like to keep stored in the space. The following systems might be helpful.

CLOSET DOOR The closet door is valuable real estate. Use adhesive hooks or over-the-door systems to hang your robe or towels. You can also hang a mesh shoe organizer over the door. These inexpensive organizers work great for bottles, cleaners, and brushes.

CONTAINERS Contain products using clear shoe boxes and labels. Consider these categories:

- ☐ First aid
- ☐ Ice packs and heating pads
- ☐ Manicure and pedicure kits
- ☐ Travel accessories
- ☐ Dental
- ☐ Shaving
- ☐ Lotions
- ☐ Cotton swabs
- ☐ Feminine products
- ☐ Hair care (bobby pins, hair ties)
- ☐ Bath items

117

MAKE YOUR OWN NATURAL CLEANING SOLUTIONS

Chemicals are everywhere, but it's not hard to cut down on the ones used in your home if you hunt around for alternatives. Whip up these natural cleaners for each area of the bathroom. They work just as well as the chemical-laden ones, but you'll feel a lot better about your chores—and the results!

SINKS Sprinkle baking soda around the sink and scrub with a wet sponge. Or mix a solution of 1 cup vinegar, 2 cups water, and 10 drops lemon or lavender essential oil to create a multipurpose cleaner. Be careful not to use vinegar on natural stone (follow the manufacturer's directions).

SHOWERS Use a damp cloth soaked with vinegar to clean shower doors. Finish with a dry microfiber cloth. Scrub shower walls with a wet sponge covered with essential oil–infused baking soda to loosen soap scum. Add a drop of liquid Castile soap for extra cleaning power. You can also make a divine-smelling daily shower cleaner by mixing together 1 cup vinegar, 2 cups water, ½ cup rubbing alcohol, 10 drops peppermint essential oil, and 10 drops orange essential oil in a spray bottle. Spray down showers daily to keep soap scum at bay. (For best results, begin with a clean shower when using daily shower cleaner. Be careful to avoid oil-rubbed bronze fixtures, as vinegar can cause damage to the finish).

TOILETS Sprinkle baking soda into the toilet, spray a generous amount of full-strength vinegar around the toilet bowl, and let it sit for several minutes. Scrub with a toilet brush. You can also use an old pumice stone—it works great for toilet stains.

From Toni

Nikki Boyd shares fantastic tips on organization, home decor, crafting, home entertaining, and more at her website athomewithnikki.com.

NIKKI, **AT HOME WITH NIKKI**

❝ Our powder room was the victim of being built with only builders' grade materials, which meant it had absolutely no character. When my husband and I purchased our home, we knew it would immediately need a makeover. The room was super small, with very high ceilings, no storage, and poor lighting. We decided to embark on the DIY project of installing beadboard wainscoting. This, along with painting the walls a beautiful gray color, gave the room an immediate uplift. We added storage by installing simple floating shelves, and we upgraded the fixtures, lighting, and mirror. Our powder room now has the storage, function and style we love! ❞

BEFORE

AFTER

WEEK 10
THE BATHROOM
Challenge

BATHROOMS TEND TO NEED cleaning more than they need organizing, as they don't accumulate too much clutter—except when it comes to all those products. The drawers and cabinets of our bathrooms inevitably end up hiding a whole lot of things that need sorting—everything from makeup and hair accessories to first-aid supplies. And we haven't even discussed the various shampoos, conditioners, hair dyes, and other bath and body products that collect in this space. Be ruthless in sorting things out—you really don't need those 15 miniature lotions you've picked up at hotels over the years!

THE PROCESS

1. PREPARE
Gather your four trusty baskets: Keep, Trash, Donate, and Other Room. There may not be a lot of "other room" stuff in the bathroom, but you should consider moving your medications. Medications that are still in use should be stored in the kitchen, not the bathroom, as many can be damaged by heat and steam (see item 039). Anything expired or that no one is taking anymore should be discarded properly (ask your pharmacy for instructions, as some medicines should not go into the landfill or down the toilet).

2. SORT AND PURGE
Go through everything in the drawers and closets and on the counters. Really scrutinize each of your bath and body products. If you keep makeup in the bathroom, look at every item and decide whether you really ever use it, or if it should be trashed. Same with hair and body products. As for the "Donate" basket: women's shelters often need shampoos and conditioners, so if you have those single-size bottles from hotels, or any products you haven't opened but don't need, consider donating them.

3. CLEAN
Give that bathroom a thorough cleaning: scrub the bath, shower, toilets, counters, mirror, and cabinets. Finish by mopping the floor, and launder any throw rugs, towels, curtains, and decorative linens.

4. ORGANIZE
Use small bins, baskets, and trays everywhere you can to group like items together. Use drawer organizers or dividers in any available spaces to keep small items contained and organized.

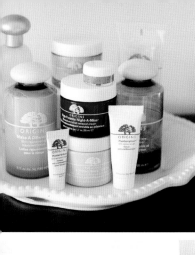

Working+Outdoor

A home that implements essential organizing systems simply functions better. As we move on to our final section, we will tackle the remaining areas of the home. I will share valuable tips on how to organize the office, including preparing for tax season and establishing a filing system, and sorting and structuring craft areas, play spaces, the laundry room, the attic and basement, and, finally, outdoor areas, including the deck, garage, and car. These can be some of the more daunting spaces to organize, but conquering these problem areas will eliminate stress as you replace the chaos and clutter with smarter solutions. Clear it, clean it, and contain it—and soon you'll have transformed the room from overwhelming to order. Dare to redefine your home and fully commit. I believe you can do it, and so should you!

Always keep your beautiful imagination & exquisite humor

118
DIVIDE YOUR OFFICE INTO ZONES

The home office is a versatile and multiuse workhorse of a room, responsible for everything from bills to day jobs to blogger duties! With so much going on and the amount of time you're likely to spend in this space, you'll want to set up an organized room that will stay that way. Here's how to divide the space into useful zones.

A. WORK ZONE The work zone is the desk area. It includes your computer, lamp, printer, tax organizer, and desktop files (these are your most-used papers that won't stay in a drawer long enough to live there).

B. MAIL ZONE Organize your mail in a drawer near your work zone. This area should include a bin for incoming and outgoing mail, as well as stamps, envelopes, address labels, packing tape, a postage scale, a stationery set, and any other correspondence needs.

C. BILL PAYMENT ZONE All things needed to pay bills go in the bill payment zone. This likely includes the bills themselves, a calculator, your checks, a budget binder, and an account and password log.

D. FILING ZONE Your filing cabinet (a paragon of home organization!) goes in the filing zone, as expected.

E. PLANNING ZONE The planning zone provides a home for any family calendars, personal organizers or planners, and other supplies (extra inserts, stickers, washi tape, etc.).

F. OFFICE SUPPLY ZONE The supply zone holds extra printer paper, printer ink, pens and pencils, staples, tape, file folders, labeler and label tape, and other office needs.

G. BOOK ZONE Even if you have bookshelves in other parts of your home, some books (personal finance, household planning, maybe even this one) may wind up on the bookshelf in your office.

H. SCHOOL ZONE The school zone includes any school paperwork and can also incorporate a homework station (see item 124).

119
CONTROL PAPER CLUTTER

Paper clutter is the number-one problem of messy home offices and it can be overwhelming and daunting to tackle. But once you get a handle on it, maintaining paper clutter is a breeze. Take control of incoming paper with a daily systematic process. As soon as paper comes into your home, take the following actions.

JUNK MAIL Immediately recycle or shred any junk mail. Don't give it a chance to accumulate—it's called junk for a reason.

BILLS Decide if you need to pay the bill now. If not, place it in a bill organizer.

KEEPSAKES If you deem a paper keepsake worthy, place it in a designated box (see item 120).

SCHOOL School papers can take over your home in an instant. Prevent this from happening by taking five minutes each afternoon, as soon as the kids get home from school, to go through each of their backpacks. Respond to any items that need your attention, recycle any trash, file artwork (see item 120), and have your children get started on their homework.

MAGAZINES & NEWSPAPERS Keep only the most current periodicals in your home. Read the daily newspaper, then place it in a designated recycling basket. If you don't have time to read it, recycle it—it's old news. Once a new magazine arrives in the mail, toss the last edition.

ACTION ITEMS Anything that needs your attention or response (such as any wedding or party invitations) should go into an action folder. Once or twice a week, go through the folder and do what needs doing.

TO FILE Important papers that need to be filed should go into a "to file" folder—but only if you don't have time to file them right away. Then once a week, go through and file everything in this folder in its proper place.

120
CREATE A KEEPSAKE BOX

When you have kids, the artwork, paperwork, pictures, and keepsakes are guaranteed to pile up. You want to wrap up their memories and cherish them forever, but it can be difficult to keep them all corralled and organized. It's essential to set up an organized system so you can file away the keepsakes in an orderly fashion. As years pass, you'll be able to look back through the memories with ease—and the good stuff won't be lost in the shuffle. Gather your supplies and adjust the categories as they apply to your family.

YOU'LL NEED

- [ ] Large filing boxes with lids (one for each child)
- [ ] Hanging file folders
- [ ] Labeler (to create labels on the hanging folders)

CATEGORIES

- [ ] Birthday cards
- [ ] Report cards
- [ ] Artwork
- [ ] School pictures
- [ ] Toddler
- [ ] Preschool
- [ ] First–twelfth grades (one file for each year)
- [ ] Academic awards
- [ ] Athletic awards
- [ ] Dance/cheer/gymnastics (or other hobby/extracurricular)
- [ ] Sports
- [ ] Theater
- [ ] Miscellaneous awards

121
ORGANIZE YOUR FILES

If you are the type of person who likes the feel of thumbing through papers and filing away work, you'll appreciate a well-organized filing system. If, instead, you are up to speed on digital record-keeping and own a document scanner, then digital file organization is the way to go. Whichever you choose, keep a handle on paperwork by taking action as soon as it arrives. Look over all documents and statements to make sure they are correct. Then shred anything you have online access to, or file away those items that you want to keep on hand. Set up a filing system using color-coded hanging folders (see item 122), and maintain it by purging irrelevant documents at least once a year (before tax season is a good time).

122
FOLLOW THE SYSTEM

Your household filing system will encompass just about everything that accumulates in a home. I recommend the following color-coded filing system sections—adjust these categories to suit your family and lifestyle.

BILLS & BANKING: *GREEN*
I highly recommend switching to online bill pay and paperless statements. However, if you do not utilize these options, you can still keep track of paper documents. Set up bills and banking into green file folders using the following subsections:
- All bills (account folders)
- Monthly folders for paid bills (January–December)
- One folder for each credit card company
- One folder for each loan (auto, mortgage, etc.)
- Paid off (any letters from loans and purchases that are paid off)
- One folder for each bank or savings account

TAXES & INCOME: *ORANGE*
Visit irs.gov to figure out how long to keep tax-related documents. Divide taxes and income documents into the following orange file folders:
- All current-year tax-related documents (one folder for each: deductions, donations, office expenses, travel expenses, etc.)
- All work-related folders (one for each job)
- Annual tax paperwork (one folder for each year).
- Retirement (401K, Roth IRAs, other investments)

MEDICAL, DENTAL, & PETS: *RED*
Organize all health and veterinary documents into red file folders as follows:
- Doctor bills (paid)
- Benefits summaries
- One medical and dental folder for each family member
- Prescriptions
- Veterinary (one folder for each pet)

HOUSE & AUTO: *YELLOW*
Keep track of home and automobile documents using yellow file folders:
- Homeowners' insurance policy
- Auto insurance policy
- House documents (paperwork pertaining to the house you currently live in)
- Homeowners' association docs
- House-related warranties
- One folder for each automobile
- Contractors (one folder for each: painting, landscaping, pool, and any other projects)

MEMBERSHIPS, SCHOOL, VACATION, & OTHER: *BLUE*
Designate one blue folder for each of the following categories:
- Schools and universities
- Clubs or memberships (YMCA, zoo, gym, aquarium)
- Cities you frequently travel to (hotel receipts, tourist activities, guidebooks, etc.)
- AAA, Sam's Club, Costco, hotel rewards, and other memberships
- Any other categories you need

123
PREP FOR TAX SEASON

It's time to get your taxes filed. So what do you need to take to your meeting with a tax pro? Obviously, a lot depends on where you live and what you do for a living. For those of us in the U.S., here's my checklist.

PERSONAL INFO

☐ Taxpayer number—your Social Security card (SSN) or individual taxpayer identification number (ITIN)

☐ Home address and county

☐ Dependent information (full legal name, date of birth, Social Security number)

DOCUMENTS

☐ W-2 for each job held during the tax year

☐ 1099 for all other income reported to the IRS, including dividend income (1099-DIV), interest income (1099-INT and 1099-OID), merchant card and third party network payments (1099-K), miscellaneous income (1099-MISC), retirement plan distribution (1099-R), sale of home or real estate (1099-S), unemployment compensation (1099-G), state tax refund, unemployment, Social Security, health-care reimbursement, and gambling winnings

☐ 1098 for payments you've made (property taxes, student loans)

☐ 1095-A if you received credit from the federal health insurance marketplace

☐ Income or interest statements received from savings accounts or investments

☐ Last year's tax return

☐ Bank account numbers and, if you wish to receive your refund by direct deposit, a voided check

☐ Record of estimated tax payments made

ITEMIZED DEDUCTIONS

☐ Education expenses including scholarships, student loan interest, and itemized receipts of qualified educational expenses (form 1098-T)

☐ Child and dependent care expenses including name, address, and tax ID or SSN of the childcare provider

☐ Business expenses and assets for self-employed individuals

☐ Educator expenses for teachers

☐ Charitable contributions—a detailed list of donations, with receipts for contributions over $250 USD

☐ Vehicle sales tax paid, personal property tax statement for each car, and total miles driven for personal use or business (keep a detailed log of miles driven for business)

☐ Homeowners info, including mortgage interest statements (form 1098), real estate taxes paid, and statement of property tax payable in tax year

☐ Retirement/IRA information, including amounts contributed to an IRA and total value as of December of tax year

☐ Moving expenses

☐ Alimony expenses, including ex-spouse's full name and SSN

☐ Health-care expenses

☐ Energy-saving home improvement documentation

☐ Foreign taxes paid

☐ First-time homebuyer documents and information

☐ Casualty and theft losses

☐ Last year's tax preparation fees

This list is an overview of the most used tax deductions and documents. Always refer to the IRS website for the complete list. You can also visit abowlfulloflemons.net to print out this checklist.

TRACK YOUR TAXES

Create file folders (using the categories listed) to keep track of your taxes during the year. Place the file folders in a mobile file box and keep the box within arm's reach of your work area. If it's out of sight, your paper will surely pile up, so placement is key!

Take advantage of forgotten spaces like the sides of cabinets and underneath desks. 3M Command hooks are the perfect alternative to putting nails in the wall.

THE OFFICE
Challenge

Office spaces can be challenging, as organizing can mean sorting through a lot of paperwork, but the effort pays off big time. If you don't have an office per se, go ahead and tackle the place where you keep your paperwork, files, important documents, mail, and other papers.

THE PROCESS

1. PREPARE
Get together six large bins or boxes, and label them as follows: Shred, File, Trash, Donate, Keep, and Other Room.

2. SORT THE PAPERWORK
Give yourself at least two hours to go through your paperwork—all of it! All papers should be sorted into one of the following bins: Shred, File, or Trash. You are not organizing at this time—just separating.

3. SORT EVERYTHING ELSE
Go through everything else in your office space. If it doesn't belong, place it in the "Other Room" bin. Once you're done, everything that isn't a piece of furniture or electronics should be in one of your bins or boxes.

4. CLEAN
Give the space a thorough cleaning. Wipe down your desk, shelves, and any electronics (carefully!), and then sweep, vacuum, and mop the floor. Be sure to clean cabinets, windows, doors, doorknobs, and light fixtures, as well.

5. FILE
Now you can organize all that paperwork into a filing system. I've found that approximately 50% of the papers you have now should probably be tossed. For each piece, ask yourself:

☐ Do I need to keep this (tax documents, birth certificates, etc.)?

☐ Will I need it in the future?

☐ Do I have a place for it?

☐ Do I have to keep it as a physical object, or can I scan it and save it on a hard drive or in the cloud?

If you answer no to all of these questions, toss it! Scan anything that you might need but don't need on paper, and shred anything that contains personal information.

6. ORGANIZE
Create a mail station to keep incoming paper from overwhelming you again after all this hard work. Then organize everything else by category. Use bins, office organizers, and trays as much as possible to keep things orderly. Likely categories are books, pens and pencils, and basic office supplies such as paper clips, sticky notes, printer ink, and so on.

SCHOOL HOUSE

EVENTS BLOG MY BOOK

TO DO MENU PLANNING

toni'sCHECKLIST

Office

Always keep your beautiful imagination & exquisite humor.

MAKE EACH DAY COUNT ...in COLOR

DECOR GARDENING HEALTH

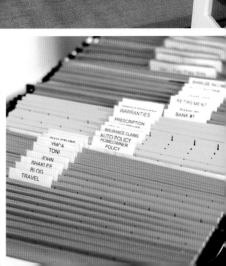

WARRANTIES

PRESCRIPTION

INSURANCE CLAIMS
AUTO POLICY
HOMEOWNER
POLICY

RETIREMENT

BANK #1

YMCA

TONI

JOHN

SHAKLEE

BLOG

TRAVEL

Tuck a homework station into a little-used closet by removing the doors, adding some chalkboard paint, and embracing a new nook.

Quick Tip

BINDER IT

Take ten minutes to create a parent's school binder to keep track of important paperwork needed throughout the year. Make a separate tab for each of the following:

- ☐ Yearly school calendar
- ☐ School information (address, phone number, principal, etc.)
- ☐ Teacher information (name and contact info, phone number, e-mail address, etc.)
- ☐ Lunch schedules
- ☐ Bell schedules
- ☐ Bus schedules
- ☐ Sick notes
- ☐ Handbook and policies

124
CREATE A HOMEWORK CENTER

A homework station is a great idea if you have school-aged children. It allows them to complete their schoolwork and study for upcoming tests in a comfortable and quiet area, and work on any projects with all of the necessary tools at their disposal. This area should be set up a good distance from distractions (like the television) and away from loud areas.

YOU'LL NEED

- ☐ Desk and chair
- ☐ Lamp
- ☐ Computer and printer
- ☐ Calculator
- ☐ Ruler
- ☐ Hanging calendar
- ☐ Crafting supplies (kept in a separate box)
- ☐ School supplies (see list)

SCHOOL SUPPLIES

- ☐ Highlighters
- ☐ Pens and pencils
- ☐ Paper stored in a desktop file box (graphing, wide- and college-ruled, construction, printer, sketch)
- ☐ Markers, colored pencils, crayons
- ☐ Glue
- ☐ Scissors
- ☐ Protractor

Set up the desk against a wall or window with good light and an even writing surface. Make sure there are enough power outlets for all the electronics and that the chair can move easily on the floor surface. Set up a few cubbies, paper trays, and stacking pencil cases to hold extra supplies and keep things as tidy as possible.

If your kitchen setup allows, you might want to designate a quiet corner for the homework center. This way, you can keep an eye on computer use and homework progress while making dinner.

125
CREATE A HOME OFFICE COFFEE STATION

If you work from home, you probably spend a lot of time in your office. The convenience of having a coffee station in this area will bring you immense joy—trust me. You can use a cute old vintage cart—or a shiny new one.

YOU'LL NEED

☐ Towels or cleaning wipes for any spills

☐ Coffee maker (the pod or K-cup kind)

☐ Wooden sticks or spoons

☐ Sugar and dry creamer, or whatever fixings you prefer

☐ Flavored syrups

☐ K-cups or coffee pods

☐ Coffee mugs or disposable cups

☐ Water bottles, juice, tea, and other favorite shelf-stable coffee alternatives

126
LOCK IN A LIBRARY

For the bookworms out there, an at-home library is a dream come true—and it doesn't necessarily require a free room. All you need is a corner of the office (or living room, or even hallway), a few pieces of furniture, and your favorite books. Place two (or more) matching bookshelves against an empty bit of wall, tuck them behind a sofa, nestle them into a corner, or mount open shelving on an odd wall space. Plop your comfiest armchair next to a bright, focused floor lamp, or set up a small table and a few chairs for a work surface. In a small home, mount narrow shelves in a long hallway, and add a window seat for a space-saving option in a little-used area. Now it's time to brush up on the Dewey Decimal System.

127
CORRAL CRAFT SUPPLIES

Crafting supplies are the hardest things to organize and keep organized. If you're lucky enough to have a designated craft room, you've fought half the battle by carving out the space—but either way, you're probably dealing with piles of scrapbook paper, yarn, sewing patterns, art supplies, or quilting fabric. Get control of your craft supplies by purging what you no longer use and implementing a category system for the rest. Whether you have an entire room or simply a closet, the organization will be the same.

CLEAN AND PURGE Start by clearing out the space completely. During this process, purge the things you no longer use or need. Don't organize clutter—get rid of it! Once the space is clear of stuff, give it a good cleaning.

LABEL AND ORGANIZE After you clean, it's time to set up your systems. There are so many ways to organize a craft space, so choose what fits your style and go with it. You can use wicker baskets, plastic shoeboxes, mason jars, glass cookie jars, filing cabinets, magazine bins, or anything else that suits your fancy. Just remember to containerize! Place the empty containers on the shelves, in drawers, and inside of cabinets. Then label each container with the items you will be storing.

PURGE & PUT AWAY After your categories and containers are in place, it's time to bring back your craft supplies. When putting supplies away, purge anything you missed during the first go-round.

128
BUILD A GIFT-WRAPPING STATION

If you happen to have the extra space (and love gift-giving), a gift-wrapping station is a wonderful thing to add to your craft room or home office. Think about the holiday season, wedding season, baby showers—and if you have kids, they will probably be invited to over a hundred parties and celebrations over the years (give or take a few). Trust me, it adds up. Being prepared will save you time, money, and headaches—and wrapping gifts will become less of a chore. It's simple and fun to build.

First, pick a place to set up your station. It doesn't have to take up a ton of room, and it doesn't have to

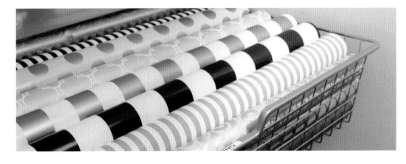

be permanently installed, either. Set one up inside a cabinet or closet or on top of a dresser with a free drawer or two. You could pack up a mobile station in a few shallow, flat boxes under the bed, or grab a free table in the garage or basement (away from prying eyes!). Then grab some clear plastic boxes and label them by category:

- ☐ Ribbon and bows (you may need multiple boxes, as bows can take up a surprising amount of space)
- ☐ Tape, scissors, and glue
- ☐ Pens and markers
- ☐ Greeting cards (sort them by occasion: birthday, sympathy, wedding and anniversary, holidays, blank, etc.)
- ☐ Gift bags
- ☐ Tissue paper

Store those gangly wrapping paper tubes in a drawer, a long and narrow plastic bin, or in a plastic organizer. A spare trash can, basket, or umbrella stand can also work wonders. Stick it in a free corner near your station. Gift boxes and bags may need larger plastic bins, as well—or might fit alongside the wrapping paper. Find what works for you, and enjoy your pro setup.

From Toni
Neat Method is a nationwide residential organizing business. To learn more about them, visit their website at neatmethod.com.

MOLLY & ASHLEY, NEAT METHOD

66 Craft closets are tricky to complete because they often have a variety of objects (big and small) that need to be stored in a way that keeps the creativity flowing. In this space, there was plenty of room to work with, but no rhyme or reason as to why things were in the places that they were. We decided it was best to start from scratch and pull everything out. An extra challenge? We were unable to make any holes in the walls! So we stuck with Expedit shelving from Ikea in one closet and an InterMetro shelving unit from the Container Store in the other. The key to the perfect craft space is to use storage solutions that are easy to see into—so that you'll be inspired to use all of the materials. Our favorite part of the project was using mason jars to store all of the beads. It made the beads easy to see and was aesthetically pleasing for the finished product. 99

BEFORE

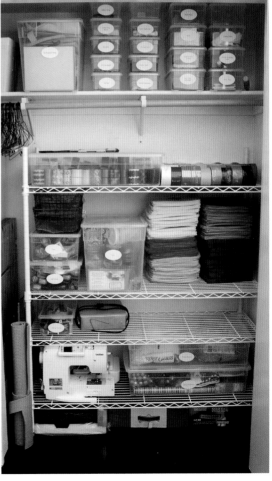

129
CREATE A TINY HOME OFFICE

In even the smallest home, the creative problem-solver can find some office space. Think about what you need—will you be using the area to pay bills and check e-mail, or to run a home-based business? The first can be done in a lot less space, but anything's possible. Here are some options to get you thinking.

BE MY GUEST Set up your office in the guest room. Keep desktop items minimal, so that it's easy to clear out when company arrives.

CREATE A CORNER Even the smallest apartment has an underutilized corner somewhere. You can set up a small desk facing into the corner and use vertical space (hanging racks, floating shelves) to minimize the footprint.

HIT THE HALL A hall that's long and not too narrow can probably accommodate a slim desk and some storage bins. The chair tends to be the thing most likely to get in the way, so use an easy-to-tuck-away stool, or borrow a kitchen chair when needed.

BOOK A NOOK Many homes have odd nooks or alcoves. Fit a small desk and some vertical storage into one of these spaces, and hang a curtain over it when not in use.

CONVERT A CLOSET Make your own nook by removing the rod from a closet. Then you can close the door and hide your office away when not in use.

Quick Tip

LET IT ROLL

Consider using a rolling storage unit with an attractive wood top as a mobile office. You can store your supplies in it, use the top as a desk when needed, then stash it all and roll the unit to the living room to use as an end table.

130
ORGANIZE KIDS' PLAY SPACES

Kids love to have their own space, and organizing their play area is a perfect activity to do together. Since it involves their toys and their designated space, they'll want to be part of the process. And besides teaching them the value of cleaning up after themselves, it's a great opportunity to reinforce learning activities such as sorting, counting, sharing, and grouping. Here are a few areas to set up.

DESIGNATE ACTIVITY STATIONS Set up an easel and paints on an easy-to-mop floor, put games on a table surrounded by cushions, and clear a flat surface for playing with blocks. Think about how the space will be used, and plan accordingly.

STORE ACCORDING TO AGE Younger children like to open bins and boxes on lower levels, while older children can use drawers, shelves, and closets. Try to keep everything within easy reach.

USE PICTURE LABELS For kids that can't quite read yet, use photographs of a container's contents. You can either use instant film, print out some digital snaps, or cut images out of magazines.

AVOID USING LARGE BOXES Toys buried at the bottom that cant' be seen rarely get played with. Keep your kids' toys grouped by type and in labeled or clear bins.

ENCOURAGE IMAGINATION Put your old scarves, hats, gloves, costume jewelry, and other fun items into a basket to encourage dress-up play.

KEEP BOXES AROUND THE HOUSE FOR EASY TRANSFERS Even if you are fortunate enough to have a separate area where your kids play, toys have a way of showing up in the darndest places. Keeping a bin handy will make the nightly toy roundup a snap.

131
ENFORCE A NIGHTLY CLEANUP

Children need to be reminded that cleaning up isn't a chore—instead, it's another way to make playing more fun. Put on a favorite song and have the kids gather and put away toys until it's over; or, while watching a favorite show, have them clean up during the commercials. Turning cleanup into an enjoyable activity will give children pride in their space and establish a routine.

BOARD THE GAMES

Store board games separately from other toys. We keep ours under the playroom coffee table. When the kids want to play a game, it's right below the table they are going to play on. It's convenient and simple organizing.

SEWING

TAPE & STICKERS

DRAWING BOOKS · COLORING BOOKS · BLANK PAPERS

CRAFT SUPPLIES

PLAY-DOH

ACTIVITY BOOKS · ACTIVITY BOOKS · STICKER BOOKS

132
TIDY UP THE PLAYROOM

The main room where your kids play with their toys can become a war zone if you don't get control of the clutter. Find a system that works and stick to it. The nightly cleanup (see item 131) will go more smoothly if you keep your organizational systems in check. Make the system work for you by remembering these key points.

LABEL Label your bins, boxes, or baskets clearly—with words or pictures, depending on your children's ages. If kids see what's supposed to go inside, they are more likely to organize correctly.

USE LIDS Our old toy organization system used open bins without lids, which works for some families, but can run into one problem: when it's time to clean up, some kids will just throw the toys into the closest bin, not the designated one, and soon the baskets are overflowing. You can find boxes with lids just about anywhere, and this small investment will save you so much time in the future.

REORGANIZE Reorganize the bins about once a month. No matter what you do or how many lids you have, a stray toy or two will inevitably get thrown into the wrong bin—and before you know it, the box labeled Barbies is now everything but Barbies.

KEEP IT SIMPLE Kids need simple!

133
PIECE THE PUZZLES

Puzzles can get out of control so quickly—and the many different sizes of boxes can be a pain to organize. To keep things stackable (and prevent lost pieces!), grab some small lidded containers and transfer each puzzle to a separate box. Cut out the picture of the finished puzzle from the box (there's usually a small one as well as the big cover shot) and throw it in with the puzzle pieces or tape it to the lid.

134
STACK A PLAY TABLE

If you're short on space but want a place for your kids to play with art supplies, puzzles, and games on their own, use flat-topped rolling storage cubes to create a piece-by-piece table that can be stored at the sides of a room.

You can attach casters to existing storage cubes, or grab some wheeled ones—you'll want a matching set of two or four, and make sure there are no overhanging lips or 3D details that would prevent them from nesting next to each other smoothly. Attach some heavy-duty Velcro strips to the corresponding sides of each cube, and put some brightly colored labels on the four corners that will meet in the middle.

Store the cubes along the perimeter of the room when not in use—they can hold games, bins, or books—and roll them together when your kids want a workspace.

135
NET A ZOO

A homemade or store-bought hanging hammock is the perfect place to keep stuffed animals—it makes it easy to put away the toys (don't hang it too high!) and it feels like a home or bed where the animals go to sleep at night. If you're a knitter, whip one up with some spare yarn and chunky needles, or simply string up some spare fabric or tulle in a storage corner. You'll save valuable floor space, to boot.

136
PITCH A TENT

If your home doesn't have a separate room available for all of the toys, Legos, games, dolls, puzzles, and everything else, there are plenty of ways to separate out some kid-safe space.

One enchanting method is to rig up a semipermanent tent in a corner of the living room, den, bedroom, or even office—wherever you have the floor space. Purchase a premade model, or simply stretch some lightweight fabric between a couple of extra chairs and add colorful streamers or fabric strips. String up some battery-powered LED twinkle lights (that don't get hot) for extra charm.

Now you have a cozy play space for young kids, and it will keep the toys and accessories neatly tucked away and out of sight.

Quick Tip

LEARN YOUR ABCS

If you have children the right age for this exercise (and enough storage space), label each bin with a letter of the alphabet and sort toys accordingly. It's a learning tool and organizational system in one!

THE PLAYROOM
Challenge

Playrooms can get messy fast, as kids love to leave their toys and games everywhere. A good organizational system will make cleaning up easier for you—and also for them. If you don't have a dedicated playroom, use this challenge to organize toys and games wherever they're kept. And if you don't have kids, focus on sorting your memorabilia, awards, and hobby or crafting supplies. This might include sporting equipment, jerseys, and pennants; any plaques or trophies; or knitting, scrapbooking, and sewing supplies—whatever items that may stack up around hobbies and collectibles.

THE PROCESS

1. PREPARE
Gather up your faithful bins, labeling them with four basic categories: Keep, Donate, Trash/Recycle, and Other Room.

2. SORT AND PURGE
Go through everything on the shelves and floors, and in baskets, toy boxes, and drawers, sorting into your bins. Purge as much clutter as you can. If your kids haven't played with something in a while or they've outgrown it, let it go. And if a certain game or toy is a major source of clutter, you might want to purge it outright. No need to break any hearts—but maybe put it out of sight for a month. If none of the kids ask for it in that time, they probably never will.

3. CLEAN
Wipe down shelves and clean all toy bins inside and out. Clean toys that just need a wipe-down, and wash stuffed animals on the gentle cycle (check care tags to be sure they won't get damaged).

4. ORGANIZE
Now it's time to go through everything in the "Keep" bin. Go through one item at a time, sorting by type of toy. Put like toys in bins together where possible, and label them for easy use. The actual categories will depend on how old your kids are and what they're into, but might include some of the following: Play Food, Arts & Crafts, Barbies, Xbox, Wii, Legos, Board Games, Stuffed Toys, American Girls, and so on.

137
LOVE THE LAUNDRY

Is your laundry room (or closet, or corner) a catch-all place? It's time to get organized, right down to the dust bunnies. Wherever your washer and dryer live, the space should be clutter-free and functional. You'd be surprised how pleasant laundry can be when the space is easy on the eyes—and efficient for the user.

Try not to keep piles of laundry in the laundry room. Keep hampers in each bathroom or bedroom, instead, and move them in when it's laundry day. If you store other household items in the laundry room, stay organized by keeping them in check—I use two white shelving units from Ikea to hold the wide variety of things that can accumulate for homekeeping. Here are some of the items that live there:

☐ Tissues

☐ Paper towels

☐ Toilet paper

☐ Sewing items

☐ Lightbulbs

☐ Tools

☐ Cat litter

☐ Cleaning wipes

☐ Floor cleaners

☐ Extra laundry detergent, soaps, and dryer sheets

138
THINK OUTSIDE THE SHOE BOX

An over-the-door shoe organizer can hold so much more than shoes. It's perfect for holding spray bottles and cleaners—keeping them out of the way but visible, so you always know what you have. Plus, you can keep dangerous chemicals out of reach. In the slim space behind the door, store your broom, mop, dusters, and ironing board, along with all your ironing tools.

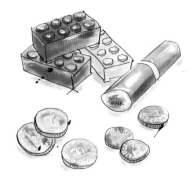

139
SET UP FORGET-ME-NOTS

Set up a few baskets or containers to hold lost items found in pockets and left behind in the dryer. Give them some labels so your family always knows where to find the lost coins, lip balms, and spare buttons.

Quick Tip

MARK A MEMENTO

I added a personal touch to my laundry room by hanging a family picture inside a vintage frame. It warms up the space and adds some visual interest.

140
WASH WITH CARE

If you really want your laundry room to be a haven, decorate! Organizing and staying efficient will only be aided by your enjoyment of the room as a whole. You're making it more usable by making it a place you want to be (and maybe laundry won't feel like such a chore for other family members, too).

The top shelf in my laundry room is more for decoration than anything, but I love it. I keep a mop bucket and some cleaning tools up there. I also love my small accessory bins for the laundry miscellany. I might not need these items every day, but they're good to have handy:

- ☐ Washing machine cleaner
- ☐ Trash bags
- ☐ Cleaning cloths
- ☐ Mopping pads
- ☐ Cleaning tools
- ☐ Sponges
- ☐ Dryer sheets
- ☐ Litter liners
- ☐ Vacuum bags

And if you have a space that lends itself to cubby storage, you can mount curtains to hide the detergents and cleansers for a simpler overall look.

141
PREVENT DRYER DISASTERS

On some machines, you can use a dry-erase marker to jot a quick note to yourself about which items shouldn't go into the dryer. A simple "blue sweater" will remind you when switching loads to fish out that delicate blend. Test the marker on an inconspicuous part of your machine, first!

142
GO HOMEMADE

If you are looking to save some money or infuse your home with more natural cleaners, try this homemade laundry detergent. I researched many recipes and most included a few common ingredients. This recipe will make enough for about 150 loads.

YOU'LL NEED

1 (76-oz) box borax

1 (76-oz) box Super Washing Soda

1 (76-oz) box baking soda

3 bars Dr. Bronner, Kirk's Castile, Fels-Naptha, Zote, or Ivory soap (shredded)

DIRECTIONS

Mix well in a large container and cover with an airtight lid. On laundry day, add two heaping tablespoons to each load. Use less with a high-efficiency washing machine, and make sure to remove the detergent selection tray. Read your manual if you're not used to powder detergent! For a fabric softener substitute, use ¼ cup (59 ml) white vinegar. Or make reusable dryer sheets by adding a few drops of essential oil to some cotton cloths.

WEEK 13
THE LAUNDRY ROOM
Challenge

This week, I challenge you to clean your laundry room from top to bottom, finish all of the laundry, and organize the space for functionality. I love my laundry room, but that hasn't always been the case—it's taken me some time to get it just the way I like it. Tackle your laundry room this week, and you, too, can create a space that's functional and even visually appealing.

For some, this may be an easy task, but for others it will be difficult to complete, especially if there are mountains of laundry or clutter in your way. If you don't have a laundry room, use this method to clean out the area where you keep your laundry supplies.

THE PROCESS

1. PREPARE
Get four bins: Keep, Trash, Donate, and Other Room. Empty out the entire laundry room, placing items in the bins. Everything but the washer, dryer, and built-in fixtures must go. If you have any cabinets in the laundry room, empty those completely, as well.

2. SORT AND PURGE
Toss empty detergent bottles and other trash. If your laundry room has storage, it probably also has some junk drawers filled with things you didn't want to keep anywhere else. Sort these and get rid of anything nonessential. If you haven't used it in the past 12 months, toss it.

3. CLEAN
Pull out the washer and dryer and vacuum behind them. Clean out the dryer vent and wipe down the outside of the washer and dryer. Clean the inside of the washer by pouring 1 cup (0.2 liter) of bleach into the drum, then running a full wash cycle on the hottest setting (with an empty machine). Wipe down all shelving, walls, baseboards, doors, and switchplates, and clean the lighting fixtures.

4. ORGANIZE
After the laundry room is clean, it's time to put everything away. Organize your laundry supplies, using bins, baskets, and trays. Label each container.
- ☐ Laundry soap
- ☐ Stain remover tools
- ☐ Cleaning cloths
- ☐ Pet items
- ☐ Cleaners
- ☐ Trash bags
- ☐ Mopping pads
- ☐ Cleaning tools
- ☐ Dryer sheets
- ☐ Paper towels
- ☐ Vacuum bags
- ☐ Sewing supplies

5. LAUNDER
Wash, dry, fold, and put away all laundry. Finish every load!

6. DECORATE
Finally, you can decorate your laundry room to make it more inviting. This is one room in the house that's often totally utilitarian, and a little cheer can go a long way.

LAUNDRY · CLEANERS

Housekeeping · SOAPBOX

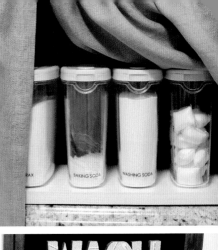

BORAX · BAKING SODA · WASHING SODA

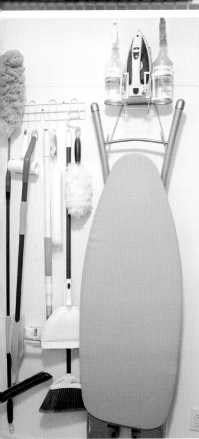

WASH

CLUB SODA · 20 MULE TEAM BORAX · NATURAL CLEANING

CLEANING CLOTHS

Quick Tip

DEAL WITH GYM ODORS

The major problem with a home gym is the funk! Here are a few things to keep in mind:

☐ Wear antiperspirant. It prevents sweating and reduces moisture.

☐ Wash your workout clothes as soon as you're finished.

☐ If your clothes really stink, soak them in vinegar before washing.

☐ Air shoes out after workouts and wash monthly.

☐ Open windows to let fresh air in.

143
SET UP A HOME GYM

If you don't have time to drive to the gym or you keep making excuses about why you never go, it's time to set up a gym in your home. You only need a few things—and you can use as few or as many of these supplies as you want. It takes less effort than you'd think to squeeze in some exercise. Here's some of the equipment I recommend.

TOWELS Stock some gym-specific regular towels and cooling towels to have on hand during workouts.

YOGA SUPPLIES You may want yoga mats, bands, blocks, and hand or foot weights.

WEIGHTS Stock free weights in various levels of heft to suit your changing requirements—and those of whoever else might want to use the space.

RESISTANCE BANDS You can hang resistance bands on wall hooks mounted into studs to keep them handy—or store them almost anywhere else (see item 145).

VIDEOS Exercise DVDs can be good motivators. Try branching out from your standard fare—workouts like ballet conditioning can be surprisingly effective.

WHITEBOARD Hang a whiteboard and stash some dry-erase markers nearby to jot down your workout schedule.

TV, TABLET, OR SPEAKERS If you like following along with instructional videos, you'll need a television or iPad to play them. If you're more of a music lover, get some good speakers or headphones to assist you with your workouts.

MACHINERY If you have the space, supplies, and inclination, find a place for your treadmill, elliptical, or other big pieces of exercise equipment. Tuck it into a corner—as long as you'll still be able to access and use it.

144
STOCK YOUR GYM BAG

Even if you don't have the luxury of a room specifically for workouts, you can take it with you via a well-stocked gym bag. You'll need these essentials when you're on the go, so keep them neatly organized and accessible in the same place. And make sure everything goes into the laundry right away!

☐ Gym shoes and extra socks

☐ Antiperspirant

☐ Travel-size body wash, shampoo, and shower shoes

☐ Towel and washcloth (if needed)

☐ Reusable water bottle

☐ Disposable bags for stinky gym clothes

☐ Earbuds and iPod

☐ Extra set of clothes

☐ Granola bar

☐ Sweat towel

☐ Hair ties and brush

☐ Lifting gloves

145
KEEP IT SIMPLE

Even if you don't have room for a treadmill, elliptical, or other piece of machinery, you'd be surprised at the kind of workout you can get using just a few space-saving resistance bands. Even the smallest home can find a corner for these multipurpose wonders. They're inexpensive, compact, and offer tons of ways to target and exercise different muscles, from bicep curls to leg lifts. It's hard to get bored when they're so versatile—and you can tailor them to your age and individual fitness level. They offer many of the same benefits as weight training—but they're a lot lighter, making them easier to move around the house or throw into a gym bag. They'll cut down on your equipment needs, and you can store them almost anywhere—hang them on the wall behind a door, fold into a box, or keep them permanently in your duffel bag. The possibilities are endless—and you might find you have room for an organized, efficient home gym, after all.

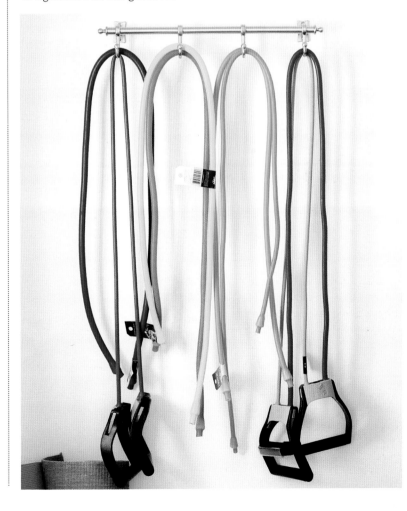

146
ATTACK YOUR ATTIC

The attic is often a place where good storage solutions go to die. But chances are your attic provides a huge amount of space that is simply going unused. It's a blank slate for any new system, won't get in anyone's way, and it's good for long-term storage. In short, it's an organizer's dream come true. If you need an attic overhaul, consider the following options.

LEAN IN If you have an attic with sloped ceilings or triangular spaces under the eaves, you can purchase (or create) specially designed storage bins with slanted sides to fit into these tricky spaces. Some can even be built into the wall or ceiling to provide extra drawer and cubby storage solutions.

EMBRACE PLASTIC Cardboard boxes, even the sturdy ones, will lose their shape and become damaged with frequent use. Instead, choose sturdy plastic containers, which provide a better seal and are easy to move from place to place.

USE THE BEAMS Those pesky exposed beams across the ceiling and up the walls can actually provide useful, efficient storage space. Make them work for you as shelves for books, which will actually benefit from being in the dark environment of many attics. No furniture or power tools required.

BEAUTIFY If your attic gets good light, let it in, clean up, and repaint. If the room looks and feels inviting, you are less likely to fill it with clutter, and you've added a new room to your house! Some attics may require a little more sweat and effort, but there's nothing like turning an unused, dusty space into a cute, useful space for your family.

147
PARE DOWN POSTERITY

Kids' art projects, old school books, former hobbies, unused sports equipment—it all finds a home in the attic. To keep the hoarding tendencies at bay, carefully sort through the whole kit and caboodle, and be strict with yourself.

KEEP Only keep important items with real sentimental value. Plan to properly archive these (which you should do now) or pass them down to the next generation. This will restrict your keepers to family heirlooms and select art or school projects that really reflect their creator (if you couldn't put them in a book and page through them in one sitting, there's too many!).

HOLIDAY If you store holiday decorations in your attic, maintain a separate section for their annual usage. But if you're keeping extras that you never actually use—like that chipped porcelain pumpkin—get them out of there.

TOSS Get rid of any damaged items that a local thrift store or donation station wouldn't accept. If they won't accept an item, then you shouldn't, either.

DONATE OR CONSIGN Donate anything you no longer use but that someone else might enjoy; consigning is a project in itself, so if you don't have the time to devote, simply donate those things, as well. You'll make someone's day when they grab it for a bargain.

148
BENEFIT FROM THE BASEMENT

Basements, especially unfinished ones, can go years without an organization plan in sight. Use zones to plan out how best to use this space. If you're lucky, you might have space for all three zones—but choose a plan that works for you.

UTILITY ZONE The utility zone of your basement is where the built-in basement trappings are located: the furnace, water heater, circuit breaker, and other household command centers. You can't always control where these are located—they might be completely spread out—so your job is to make sure they're always accessible. You'll need them in emergencies or when maintenance workers come through. Use rolling shelves if you can't avoid blocking them in.

STORAGE ZONE The storage zone will divide into smaller zones as you categorize everything that remains in the basement after you purge unnecessary items. This is the space for furniture, bicycles, tools, and vacation or camping gear.

LIVING ZONE If you have a finished section of your basement (maybe a media room or guest space), this is your living zone—somewhere the family gathers. It might also be a dedicated-use space, such as a playroom, craft space, or workshop.

149
USE FORGOTTEN SPACES

Utilize space that's often forgotten by adding storage in unexpected places. Your basement might not provide all of these options, but try to think outside the box as to how odd solutions might work for you.

STAIRS Install shelves with totes or bins underneath the basement stairs. Some staircases may even have built-in closets or cupboards that can be put to all sorts of uses.

CEILINGS If you have enough space, use overhead racks and bins to get bulky items like artificial Christmas trees or bicycles out of the way. These also work for items that don't need to be readily accessible, like those sentimental clothes and books you're saving for your grandchildren.

VERTICALS If you've ever tripped over a bike, you know that a wall-mounted bike rack is a great tool for freeing up floor space.

Quick Tip

MOUNT A FUSE BOX FLASHLIGHT

You're bound to blow a fuse at some point, so grab some Velcro or magnetic tape and mount a flashlight right next to the fuse box. You'll know where to find it the next time you're heading into the dark.

150

BUILD A MINI GREENHOUSE

In cold winter climates, you can use certain basements to extend the gardening season. A basement greenhouse can be as simple or as involved as you'd like it to be. Maybe you'd like to grow enough vegetables to feed your family all winter, or maybe you're a gardener who wants to flex your green thumb during the cold months. Either way, you probably already have plenty of pots, soil, seeds, and plants that would love to find a home for the winter.

A true greenhouse will need grow lights or shop lights, and they can be pricey (don't forget about the electric bill). But investing in a few might satisfy your gardening urge for years to come. Use the lights to help seeds germinate in midwinter, for spring and summer flowers as well as an assortment of vegetables.

Even without shop lights, an aboveground window (if your basement is elevated or your house is built into a hill) can work wonders. Many gardeners throw away their geraniums in the fall, and though they're certainly not at their best during winter, they can be kept alive in a sunny cellar window until spring. Paperwhite daffodils and amaryllis can be potted in soil or marble chips, tended in the basement while they grow, and then brought upstairs when they bloom for the holidays.

Do some research, and make your basement work for your needs.

151

KEEP BASEMENTS CLEAN AND DRY

After sorting your basement's contents and organizing everything that will be staying put for long-term storage, be smart about how you store these items. Use clear plastic containers that allow you to see what's inside, and set up a dehumidifier where possible—it will help control odors and prevent moisture buildup, which can damage your items. If you're storing furniture in the basement, drape dropcloths or blankets over them and keep them from touching the walls (which can harbor moisture). If you have an aboveground basement with windows and good air circulation, this may not be necessary. Follow your nose!

152

PRACTICE CAUTION WITH ARCHIVED ITEMS

You likely know someone who was greeted with ankle-deep water in the basement on the morning after a heavy rainstorm. Some areas are prone to flooding, and sometimes there's not much you can do about it—except protect your sentimental and valuable items. Don't set anything that could be harmed by water on the floor, and store any books, records, paper products, photos, textiles, or stuffed animals somewhere else (like the attic). If you need to put them in the basement, try ceiling-mounted racks with attachable bins, or keep them elevated with stacked cinder blocks. And stay away from cardboard containers!

153
SALVAGE A SHED

Do you have a shed filled with unused clutter? Clear it out and reinvent the space. It can become an artist's studio, man cave, gardener's shed, or even serve as extra space to store holiday decorations. Keep it simple—or get creative!

☐ Use a freestanding desk or install a countertop across the length of the back wall for maximum workspace.

☐ Hang shelving along the walls to expand storage.

☐ Install a pegboard above the desk to hang tools and supplies. Spray paint it a fun color for added pizazz.

☐ Label bins and baskets to implement order in the space.

154
GET THE HOLIDAY HOOKUP

Don't be discouraged by the daunting task of putting items like holiday lights and ornaments into storage. There are a number of ways to make the process as pain-free as possible.

Wrap Christmas lights, tinsel, and other tangle-prone garlands around plastic hangers or sturdy pieces of cardboard before putting them into storage for the next 11 months. You'll thank yourself later when trimming your tree doesn't get delayed by an hour-long detangling party. You can also buy holiday light storage reels to serve the same purpose. If you have multiple sets, label each garland with its destination to save time (for example, "banister," "porch column," "front tree").

For ornaments, store small ones in egg cartons (the sturdy plastic kind are best) or apple crates. Old wine and beer crates are also great for storing larger ornaments.

Finally, rather than searching through boxes and crates for gift-wrapping supplies that you used up last year, make a list at the end of the season of things you need to buy next year. Better yet, run out and grab them now! Those post-holiday markdowns can't be beat.

155
STORE SPLASH SUPPLIES

If you have a pool or waterway nearby, you're likely stocked to the gills with floaties, toys, swimming aids, and other accessories.

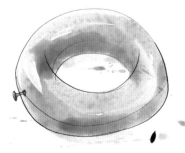

Whether you're keeping the family pool organized or corralling the various beach vacation supplies between tropical trips, keep a few things in mind.

SUNSCREEN AND SPRAYS Keep extra sunscreen and bug spray in a bucket by the pool (or near the vacation gear), in case anybody forgets to bring or pack their own. Remember to check expiration dates. (I've always liked this bit of popular wisdom: If you're not using up your sunscreen bottles before they expire, it means you're not using enough sunscreen!)

PORTABLE ORGANIZATION Mount some hooks or wire baskets to an old pallet or large piece of wood for a towel organization system that can move inside or outside as needed. Keep it in the garage when not in use or during the off season, and take it outside for the start of summer and pool parties. It can serve as a handy drying rack for wet suits and towels.

MILDEW MAINTENANCE Make sure any baskets or bins used for storage have good-sized holes or mesh in the bottom to drain water, and ensure your hooks (or any other places you store wet items) aren't too close together so that air can circulate. The key to avoiding mildew is allowing air to get in and around items. Also make sure to retire any toys that get stinky but can't go in the washing machine.

156
PERFECT YOUR PATIO

If you're lucky enough to have an outdoor space like a patio, porch, or deck for entertaining, it's time to get things in order to make sure you're ready. Whether you use your space once a season or every day, a little organization will make it more useful and enjoyable.

The perfect storage solution can sometimes be as simple as finding a new piece of multipurpose furniture to create spaces for things that were previously homeless. If you grill often, repurpose a teak ladder as a shallow shelf, and add hooks for BBQ implements or garden tools that need to be kept handy. Or use a wicker end table with a glass top to hold plants, drinks, and trays of food. A wall-mounted wire organizing rack can hold incoming mail on a front porch. Hide clutter with outdoor cabinets and storage units. There are endless options—find what works for your space.

157
GO VERTICAL

Even if you don't have a huge yard with lots of garden space, vertical patio gardening provides endless options and helps to avoid the traffic hazard that too many potted plants can cause. Incorporate vines, hanging plants, and mounted planter boxes along fences to open up walking paths and decorate the vertical surfaces.

Quick Tip

USE THE PERIMETER

L-shaped benches against the wall will keep your guests comfortable while leaving the center space free for tables, fire pits, and grills.

158
INVEST IN OUTDOOR FABRICS

Outdoor furniture is built to withstand the elements, but be careful when choosing your cushions. Even if you don't sit outside very often, you'd be surprised what wind, rain, weather, and exposure to the elements can do to even the toughest fibers. Look for outdoor furniture–specific fabrics, which generally undergo a special chemical treatment to increase moisture resistance. If needed, hose fabrics down weekly, or deep-clean with a mild soap and water. Avoid detergents and hot water, which can compromise the protective materials. Store cushions in a covered area—and if they get caught in the rain, stand them on end to help them dry more quickly.

159
OVERHAUL THE GARAGE

The garage—or any utility space—can become a storage ground for clutter that isn't even yours! If you're human, your garage is probably a mess—or you've worked hard to change it. Here are some ideas for organizational systems in this space—they may not work for every space, but try a few and find what suits your usage level.

INSTALL SHELVING Keep floors clear of clutter by installing vertical shelving systems or building your own. Choose from metal, wood, or plastic, but if you live in a humid area and your garage isn't insulated, watch out for the moisture that wood can absorb.

BUILD DRAWERS Commonly used items such as batteries, trash bags, and outdoor toys should remain easily accessible. Upcycle an old dresser and place clear shoe boxes in the drawers, or install a drawer unit for handy storage.

UTILIZE THE CEILING The ceiling is wasted space that most people don't think about incorporating into their garage storage. Hang bikes from utility hooks or add shelving over the garage door to store holiday decorations.

CONTAINERIZE Large totes fit well on most shelving units and can hold many things. Small containers are great for items such as rolls of adhesive, flashlights, tape measures, and other small tools. Categorize and containerize to keep your garage tidy.

LABEL EVERYTHING Take organization one step further and label all containers, big and small. Use a label maker, hanging tags, chalkboard paint, or a vinyl lettering machine—whatever your preferred system might be. Labeling alleviates the need to search box after box to find what you're looking for. This can be especially useful in the garage, where things can go to live for a long time before they're sought after again.

UPDATE FLOORING Complete your garage overhaul by giving the floor a fresh coat of paint. Home improvement stores carry DIY garage floor painting kits so you can tackle it yourself—or make it snappy and call in a professional.

160
FOLLOW SAFETY RULES

The garage can be a treacherous place, filled with all the flammable fuels and sharp tools that we don't want to keep in the house. Make sure you take precautions to keep everyone safe.

SAFETY GEAR Wear proper personal protective equipment (gloves, hard shoes, safety glasses, etc.) while using power tools.

SECURE SHELVING Make sure to anchor all shelving into the wall studs to prevent accidents and injuries.

HAZARDOUS ITEMS

- [ ] Store flammables and chemicals according to directions. Read warning labels carefully.
- [ ] Chemicals and paint should be secured away from children.
- [ ] Store sharps out of reach of children.
- [ ] Always keep dangerous chemicals in their original containers.

CARBON MONOXIDE DETECTOR CO is a dangerous gas and a silent killer. Install a detector in the garage to monitor the levels.

FIRE EXTINGUISHER Always keep a working fire extinguisher in the garage. They expire, so be sure to check the date, mark your calendar, and replace it when needed.

Quick Tip

STORE TOOLS

There are many ways to sort your tool storage. Mount a pegboard on the wall to neatly display tools and tidbits. Add a coat of spray paint and trim for a more custom look. Use classic mason jars for smaller items—they're perfect for just about any type of project. Display nails and screws in jam jars, feed twine through a hole in the lid, or store a dozen sticks of glue. The sky's the limit! Last but not least, stackable, clear shoeboxes can store all types of tools, sharps (such as box cutters), and other handy items.

161
STORE SEASONAL SUPPLIES

A garage is a great place to store not only tools and automotive gear, but also off-season items like sports equipment, camping supplies, gardening tools, vacation essentials, and anything else that can be put away for a long period of time.

SPORTS GEAR Rig up a few bungee cords to create a ball storage system, or throw basketballs into a net that cinches at the top. Get bats, rackets, clubs, sticks, and other gear off the floor and on the wall using hooks or brackets.

PET GEAR Large pet items like bulk food bags, bathing tools, and little-used carriers should be stored somewhere easy to access but out of the way. If you bathe your dog in a kiddie pool, use the empty plastic pool as a giant bin to corral your larger items.

VACATION AND HOLIDAY GEAR If you have the space and the ambition, install storage bins in the empty space between the open garage door and the ceiling. Measure twice—or maybe three times—and test carefully.

GARDENING AND LAWN GEAR Keep your lawnmower, weed whacker, and other machinery (and tripping hazards like rakes) away from kid-friendly zones and high-traffic pathways.

WINTER GEAR Keep snow boots, shovels, holiday decorations, and sidewalk salt in a designated area. Make sure breakable items are carefully wrapped and secured inside labeled plastic bins. Always place larger and heavier items on the bottom and lighter bins on top, and remember that overloading containers leads to dropping them!

163
CREATE A GOODBYE STATION

Set up a donation or goodbye station in your garage for any items from your home that are on their way out. This will help you keep track of these items, and remind you to take them to their assigned new (or old) homes. Separate them by category as follows:

- ☐ Donate: Any items you are donating to charity
- ☐ Return: Any store-bought items that need to be returned—make it a mission to return them all within a week!
- ☐ Sell: Anything that you will be selling in your upcoming garage sale
- ☐ Borrowed: Items that you've borrowed and need to return to their rightful owner

Get that stuff out of there, and enjoy your newly reclaimed space!

162
KEEP CLEAN

It takes a little extra effort to keep garages and other areas that see a lot of outdoor activity clean and protected from the elements. Sweep floors with a push broom and wipe down any sills and frames to keep cobwebs at bay. Clean any screens with warm water and all-purpose cleaner, using a scrub brush to get into the mesh as well as the frames. Then hose them off and allow to air dry. If you have a large deck or porch, or a drain in your garage, a power washer can be a great

investment to blast away mildew, dirt, and stains—just be sure not to use it on untreated wood. Watch for any loose nails and fill holes with putty, and make sure to reseal your deck or floors when needed. Wash light fixture covers every month, as insects tend to collect inside, and dry thoroughly before you replace them.

From Toni

Samantha Pregenzer is a professional organizer who blogs about easy projects, DIYs, organizing inspiration, products, and client projects at simplyorganized.me.

SAMANTHA, **SIMPLY ORGANIZED**

66 A cluttered garage like mine is a challenge to organize because it's essentially one big room, so you need to create zones. A garage should be treated like any other space in your home, so whatever lives in it should have meaning, serve a purpose, be useful, and have a place. During the sorting process, we decided what wasn't being used and donated duplicates. Categories naturally appeared, and once we knew what needed a home, I drafted a plan that made the most of the space, including lots of vertical storage. Get that shelving all the way to the top! It's a garage, so you don't need anything fancy, but with the correct systems in place, I was able to put everything away. It's very nice to have my neighbors admiring the space—but it's even better to be an inspired homeowner ready to take on more projects—because I can see everything! 99

BEFORE

AFTER

WEEK 14

THE GARAGE

Challenge

This is another tough one—the garage can be the hardest of all the challenges for some people—but it's so worth it.

If you're like I used to be, you save tons of things "just in case" you need them (and then never do). When we moved into our dream home, I vowed not to hoard the clutter anymore. So we purged . . . and purged some more. We got rid of a ton of stuff! Now we are at the point where we can finally manage what we own. If you're not at this point, this process will get you there.

For some readers, these tasks may be too much to handle in one week. Please don't be discouraged. Do what you can—even just tidying and sweeping will make you feel good. If you don't have a garage, tackle whatever utility storage space you use, whether it's a basement, attic, or utility closet.

THE PROCESS

1. PREPARE

Before you start, call a local charity organization and schedule an appointment for them to come with a truck and pick up your bigger donations. Many organizations schedule a week or more in advance, so get this done first. Next, be sure you have a number of big bins or boxes for sorting. Line them up in the driveway, since everything should come out of the garage to be categorized.

2. SORT AND PURGE

Go through all of your junk, one piece at a time, removing items to be trashed or donated, and organizing the rest of your stuff into the bin categories. Categories will vary depending on your lifestyle, but might include groups like sports, gardening, tools, car maintenance, painting, pets, grilling, beach or pool, and so on. Empty the garage completely, right down to the bare walls, floor, and fixtures.

3. CLEAN

Once the garage is empty, it's time to sweep, use a leaf blower, or hose down the floor, depending on how dirty your garage is. During this step, if you have a problem with spiders or ants, you can spray the perimeter of your garage with a natural pesticide. Once you return everything to the garage, try to keep it all off the ground. Spiders like to hide behind stuff—and so does dust!

4. FINISH

Now place all of your donatables together just inside the door, so you'll be ready when the charity comes, and congratulate yourself on a job well done.

164
KEEP THE CAR TIDY

Maintaining a clean car can seem impossible when we have crazy, busy days—or, of course, kids! But there are a few processes you can put in place to help keep the car tidy.

ADD A TRASH CAN Use a plastic bag to line a large plastic cereal dispenser (with a lid). Keep it in the car to use as a trash can. The lid prevents trash from spilling out and making messes, and it's way better than trash being spread across the entirety of the backseat. Empty the bag every evening.

165
STOCK THE CAR FOR EMERGENCIES

While on the go, you're bound to run into a few accidents or emergencies. Prepare ahead of time by putting together emergency kits for the car. You never know when an emergency will arise, so it's best to be ready for the unexpected. Just remember to remove temperature-sensitive items from the car during periods or seasons of extreme heat or cold.

EMPTY THE CAR OUT The number-one way to keep the car tidy is to empty it out completely every evening. Make it part of the routine for the whole family, and teach kids to be responsible for removing their own things.

ELIMINATE UNNECESSARY CLUTTER Take inventory of everything that's being kept in the car full-time. Is it all being used? Remove anything that isn't a functional part of traveling. By removing excess items, the car will stay tidy.

VACUUM & WASH There's nothing better than a sparkly clean car. Take pride in it—you spent a fortune on it! Cleaning your car is no different than cleaning your house, so keep it looking good.

EMERGENCY KITS
- ☐ Personal care kit (hand sanitizer, tissues, feminine products, lip balm, lotion, sunscreen, trash bag, water bottle, blanket, extra money, nonperishable snacks)
- ☐ First-aid kit
- ☐ Potty training kit (wipes, extra clothing, diapers, pull-ups, plastic bag)

CAR CARE KIT
- ☐ Jumper cables
- ☐ Flashlight and extra batteries
- ☐ Duct tape
- ☐ Multipurpose utility tool
- ☐ Flare lights
- ☐ Tire sealant
- ☐ Gloves
- ☐ Tow rope
- ☐ Shovel

166
ROCK YOUR ROAD TRIPS

Traveling with the family—however large or small—can be a lot of fun, or a lot of stress, and sometimes both. Equip your car to assist you in all aspects of long car rides. (You packed the emergency kit, right?)

LISTEN UP Audiobooks are a wonderful form of entertainment that everyone in the car can enjoy (even the driver). Check out a few from the library and give them a test run to see which titles and narrators hold everyone's interest.

GRAB A CADDY Shower caddies and plastic totes can serve as perfect, portable meal containers—either while munching on homemade sandwiches or after a drive-thru pit stop.

ROLL THE DICE If backseat board games or dice games are happening, pop the dice into a tiny, clear Tupperware container. They'll never get lost between the seats again.

HANG UP Cut a shoe organizer down to size, run a piece of twine through the hook, and pop it over the front seat. Your backseat passengers will have more storage than you do.

WEEK 15
THE CAR
Challenge

So, you've cleaned and organized every room in your house. What's next? Our final challenge is the car. In my opinion, our cars influence our state of mind. We're in and out of them all day, and if the car is messy, we will be more stressed and anxious. So it's amazing what cleaning out your car can do for your peace of mind. And the good news? This "room" is smaller than a lot of the other ones you've tackled over the past few weeks.

Keep your car as clutter-free and clean as possible. Vacuum and wash it weekly. You spent a lot of money on it, so you probably want it to last a long time.

One key rule for our household is that no food or drinks are allowed inside the car. Trust me, the kids will not starve if they don't eat in the car. You can make exceptions if a long road trip is involved, of course, but by having a no-food rule in our car, 75% of the mess is eliminated before it even begins.

THE PROCESS

1. PREPARE
Gather two bins and a large trash bag. The bins are for "keep in car" or "take in to house." The trash bag is for the obvious: trash!

2. SORT AND PURGE
Remove everything in the car that isn't an essential part of it. Empty it completely. Sort everything into your bins, and trash anything you really don't need. Be ruthless and remember how your car is used.

3. CLEAN
Clean your car thoroughly. Vacuum it, wipe down the inside, and take the mats out to vacuum or shampoo. Clean the windows inside and out, and wash down the car's exterior.

4. ORGANIZE
Now, go through everything in your "keep in car" bin and organize it by category. Keep like items together to stash in the trunk, central console, or glove compartment, as follows:

Trunk Stock reusable grocery bags, a car emergency kit (flares, spare fuses, jumper cables, etc.), a basic first-aid kit, and a kid kit (if you have kids, you can keep car toys together in a bag or bin).

Central console The central console can be a real clutter magnet (it's sort of the junk drawer of the car), so limit its contents to the essentials. For me, that means lip balm, wet wipes, and parking meter coins.

Glove compartment Keep a small binder of car papers in the glove box, along with any business receipts and charging cords.

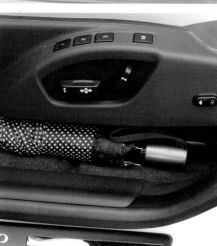

In closing

By understanding where clutter originates and the effect it has on your life, you will begin to see the importance of a regular purging schedule. Mess can manifest in so many ways, and you can rid yourself of habits to help it along. If you are planning a shopping trip, consider donating a few items beforehand instead of adding more to an already-filled space. Set aside one day a week to go through things you no longer use or need, and you'll find that purging clutter on a regular basis will ease the stress of an unbalanced home. It's the little things that make the biggest difference—in terms of getting organized in the first place, and of making sure it stays that way.

Whether you paged through this book from room to room and followed each challenge in order or combed through a few sections at a time, I hope you've gained valuable tips and ideas to bring order to your home. Face up to the mess and the clutter, establish a system, and stick to it—even the smallest projects can make a huge difference. Soon, you'll fall into patterns, and chaos will be the exception, not the rule.

Everyone is different, so figure out the best ways to make your spaces work for you—and enjoy the balance and efficiency of your newly organized, tailor-made home.

Index

Index

Index

Acknowledgments

First and foremost, I would like to give thanks to God. I am here because of His mercy and grace. I want to thank Weldon Owen Publishing for giving me such an amazing opportunity and for believing that I had the ability and vision to write this book. I want to give a very special thanks to my editor Bridget Fitzgerald, for helping me tremendously and guiding me every step of the way. I couldn't have done it without you. To my editor Mariah Bear, thank you for keeping me on track. You inspired me to continue on and push through it. I would also like to thank designer Jennifer Durrant, who graciously accepted my compulsive need to change things around throughout the entire process. And a big thanks to art director William Mack, illustrators Juan Calle and Louise Morgan, and the publicity and marketing teams, including Cathy Hebert and Molly Battles. You are all very much appreciated.

   Thank you to the rest of the Weldon Owen team, for your creative talents and hard work on this project. I give many thanks to everyone involved from the beginning to the very end.

   To the thousands of blog fans who have allowed me to share my love of organizing with the world: You are the reason why I'm still blogging five years later.

   To the top organizing bloggers who have been there since the beginning—you are all an inspiration to me. Becky Rapinchuk, Becky Barnfather, Anna Moseley, Ginny Grover, Leslie Ann Holt, Leanne Jacobs, and Laura Wittmann, I love you girls.

   To all of A Bowl Full of Lemons' Facebook communities who have shown their immeasurable love and support for my blog. I cannot thank you enough.

   Last, but certainly not least, I would like to thank my family for their unconditional love, patience, and understanding during the last several months. I apologize for the lack of home-cooked meals, clean laundry, and much-needed attention during this time. I knew you would be fine, because you are three amazing kids. I'm so proud to be your mom. Thanks to my husband for stepping in and taking over the many duties involved in being a stay-at-home mom. You were the glue that held the family together while I was overwhelmed during this journey. I'm truly thankful and lucky to have such a supportive man in my life. You are my rock and I couldn't have done it without you. I love you with all my heart.

About the Author

Toni Hammersley is the creator and writer of www.abowlfulloflemons.net, an organizing website that inspires thousands of people around the world to get their lives in order. She hosts a popular 14-week organizing challenge each year, aimed at helping others conquer clutter. She is also a registered nurse and photographer. She lives in Charleston, South Carolina with her husband and three children.

Credits

All photographs © *Toni Hammersley* except as follows. *Melanie Acevedo* (© *Weldon Owen/ Pottery Barn Kids*): 093, 094; *Lincoln Barbour*: full page across from 002, 024, 032 (top), full spread after 070, full page across from 072, full page across from 106, full page across from 123; *Amy Bartlam:* full spread after 029 (design by Kate Lester Interiors); *Alexander van Berg:* full page across from 029; *Paul Dyer Photography:* full page across from 019; *Jeff Freeman:* 008; *Scott Hargis* (*scotthargisphoto.com*): full page across from 070; Alison Hammond Photography: full page across from 126 (interior design by Egon Walesch Interiors & Flowers); *Richard Leo Johnson/ Atlantic Archives, Inc.:* full page across from 112; *Simon Kenny:* full page across from 146, 106; *Johasen Krause:* Working + Outdoor opener, 124, 156, 157; *Sean Litchfield:* full page across from 003 ; *Cindy Loughridge:* 018, 071; *Mark Lund* (© *Weldon Owen/Pottery Barn*): 119, 122, 129 (full page), 153; *David Matheson* (© *Weldon Owen/Pottery Barn*): 036; *Stefano Massei* (© Weldon Owen/Pottery Barn): 064, 068, 082, 098, 106, 140, 146 (small); *NEAT Method Photography/ Michelle Drewes:* 041, full page across from 096; *No. 29 Design:* full page across from 124; *Mirian Parsons* (*missmustardseed.com*): 057, full page across from 068, full page across from 111, full page across from 122; *Lisa Petrole:* 092; *Eric Roth:* full page across from 117, 136; *Prue Ruscoe* (© *Weldon Owen/Pottery Barn*): 077, 086; *Shutterstock:* Quick Tip next to 003, 013 (knives and pots), full spread after 018, 047, 048, 049, 050, 058, 060, 096, 105, Quick Tip next to 129, Quick Tip next to 131, Quick Tip next to 139, 150, 154,166; *Jill Sörensen:* full page across from 088; *Daniel Trovato:* full page across from 092 (design by Hide & Sleep); *Simon Whitmore:* 076: *Alan Williams:* 085; *IPC Syndication/Homes & Gardens/Polly Wreford:* 142

All illustrations courtesy of Louise Morgan except the following: *Juan Calle:* 002, 017, 052, 070, 118

Before and After images courtesy of:
Organizing Made Fun *organizingmadefun.com*
Graceful Order *gracefulorder.com*
Ask Anna *askannamoseley.com*
Organizing Home Life *organizinghomelife.com*
At Home with Nikki *athomewithnikki.com*
Neat Method *neatmethod.com*
Simply Organized *simplyorganized.me*

weldon**owen**

PRESIDENT & PUBLISHER	Roger Shaw
ASSOCIATE PUBLISHER	Mariah Bear
SVP, SALES & MARKETING	Amy Kaneko
FINANCE DIRECTOR	Philip Paulick
EDITOR	Bridget Fitzgerald
CREATIVE DIRECTOR	Kelly Booth
ART DIRECTOR	William Mack
DESIGNER	Jennifer Durrant
ILLUSTRATION COORDINATOR	Conor Buckley
PRODUCTION DIRECTOR	Chris Hemesath
ASSOCIATE PRODUCTION DIRECTOR	Michelle Duggan
DIRECTOR OF ENTERPRISE SYSTEMS	Shawn Macey
IMAGING MANAGER	Don Hill

Weldon Owen would like to thank Katharine Moore, Molly Stewart, and Jim Fitzgerald for their editorial services, and Kevin Broccoli for the index.

© 2016 WELDON OWEN INC.
P.O. BOX 3088
SAN RAFAEL, CA 94912
WWW.WELDONOWEN.COM

A BOWL FULL OF LEMONS IS © A BOWL FULL OF LEMONS, LLC.

PRINTED IN CHINA.

LIBRARY OF CONGRESS CONTROL NUMBER ON FILE WITH THE PUBLISHER.

ISBN 978-1-61628-957-7
10 9 8 7 6 5 4 3 2 1
2021 2022 2023 2024